LONGMAN PREPARATION SERIES FOR THE TOEIC® TEST

MORE PRACTICE TESTS 5TH EDITION

LISTENING AND READING

Lin Lougheed

Longman Preparation Series for the TOEIC® Test: Listening and Reading, More Practice Tests, Fifth Edition

Pearson Education, 10 Bank Street, White Plains, NY 10606

Staff credits: The people who made up the ***Longman Preparation Series for the TOEIC® Test: Listening and Reading*** team—representing editorial, production, design, and manufacturing—are Aerin Csigay, Dave Dickey, Pam Fishman, Mike Kemper, Barbara Perez, Liza Pleva, Robert Ruvo, and Adina Zoltan.

Development: Helen B. Ambrosio Publishing Services, Inc.
Text composition: ElectraGraphics, Inc.
Text font: Palatino
Cover photograph: Shutterstock.com
Cover design: Barbara Perez

Photo Credits: All photos are used under license from Shutterstock.com except for the following: **Page 3** Copyright © Educational Testing Service. Reprinted with permission; **p. 8** (top) Instructional Design International, Inc., Washington D.C.; **p. 43** Copyright © Educational Testing Service. Reprinted with permission; **p. 44** (bottom) Bob Daemmrich/PhotoEdit Inc.; **p. 47** (bottom) Instructional Design International, Inc., Washington D.C.; **p. 85** Copyright © Educational Testing Service. Reprinted with permission; **p. 86** (top) Instructional Design International, Inc., Washington D.C.; **p. 88** (top) Instructional Design International, Inc., Washington D.C.; **p. 125** Copyright © Educational Testing Service. Reprinted with permission; **p. 127** (top) Jeff Greenberg/PhotoEdit Inc.; **p. 128** (top) Instructional Design International, Inc., Washington D.C.; **p. 130** (bottom) Instructional Design International, Inc., Washington D.C.

Library of Congress Cataloging-in-Publication Data

Lougheed, Lin
Longman preparation series for the TOEIC test: listening and reading. Introductory course / Lin Lougheed.—5th ed.
p. cm.
ISBN 978-0-13-286148-9 (with answer key)—ISBN 0-13-286148-8 (with answer key)—ISBN 978-0-13-286151-9 (without answer key)—ISBN 0-13-286151-8 (without answer key)—ISBN 0-13-286142-9—ISBN 0-13-286146-1—ISBN 0-13-286152-6—ISBN 0-13-286143-7—ISBN 0-13-286145-3 1. Test of English for International Communication—Study guides. 2. English language—Business English—Examinations—Study guides. 3. English language—Textbooks for foreign speakers. I. Lougheed, Lin, 1946– Longman preparation series for the TOEIC test. Introductory course. II. Title.

PE1128.L646 2012
428.0076—dc23

2011037693

Printed in the United States of America

ISBN 10: 0-13-286149-6
ISBN 13: 978-0-13-286149-6

1 2 3 4 5 6 7 8 9 10—V001—17 16 15 14 13 12

R

CONTENTS

INTRODUCTION

GENERAL TEST-TAKING DIRECTIONS

Longman Preparation Series for the TOEIC® Test: More Practice Tests will give you the practice you need to do well on the TOEIC test. When you take the tests in this book, you should pretend that you are actually taking the TOEIC test. Make sure that you have enough time to complete each section of the test. It is not necessary to take the whole test all at once if you do not have enough time. However, you should not spend more time than is allowed for each part.

You will need a soft lead pencil and a copy of one of the answer sheets from the back of the book. All answers for the TOEIC test will be marked on a similar sheet. Do not write in your book. This will allow you to take the test more than once. When you mark your answer sheet, completely fill the oval. Do not make any marks outside of the oval. If you do not know the answer to a question, **guess.** You may guess correctly!

The answers for the Practice Tests are supplied as PDF files, and can be found in selected editions on the CD-ROM bound into this book. Each answer in the Answer Key has a short explanation. These explanations refer you to study materials found in other books in the *Longman Preparation Series for the TOEIC® Test: Listening and Reading*. These books, *Introductory Course*, *Intermediate Course*, and *Advanced Course*, are available at your bookstore or from your local Longman representative.

You will find a Conversion Table on page 176. The table will give you an approximation of what your TOEIC test scores might be. Please note that this is an approximation, not an actual TOEIC test score.

Listening Comprehension

Notice the headphone symbol used throughout the book. The symbol means you will need to listen to the audio files, located either as mp3 files in the CD-ROM bound into the back of this book, or on separately purchased audio CDs. If you do not have a method of listening to the audio, you may have someone read you the questions from the audioscript. The audioscript is included as a PDF file on the enclosed CD-ROM.

There are four parts to the Listening Comprehension section.

Listening Comprehension	Part 1 Photos	10	45 minutes
	Part 2 Question-Response	30	
	Part 3 Conversations	30	
	Part 4 Talks	30	
	TOTAL	100	

Reading

You will only need the test book, an answer sheet, and a pencil to do the Reading section. There are three parts to the Reading section of the test.

Reading	Part 5 Incomplete Sentences Part 6 Text Completion Part 7 Reading Comprehension • Single Passages • Double Passages TOTAL	40 12 28 20 100	75 minutes

TOEIC TEST DIRECTIONS

General Directions

These directions are provided by the Educational Testing Service (ETS) and are reprinted here with their permission. Read them and make sure you understand them. These directions are the same on every test.

Test of English for International Communication

General Directions

This test is designed to measure your English language ability. The test is divided into two sections: Listening and Reading.

You must mark all of your answers on the separate answer sheet. For each question, you should select the best answer from the answer choices given. Then, on your answer sheet, you should find the number of the question and fill in the space that corresponds to the letter of the answer that you have selected. If you decide to change an answer, completely erase your old answer and then mark your new answer.

PRACTICE TESTS

PRACTICE TEST ONE

You will find the Answer Sheet for Practice Test One on page 167. Detach it from the book and use it to record your answers. Play the audio for Practice Test One when you are ready to begin.

LISTENING TEST

In the Listening test, you will be asked to demonstrate how well you understand spoken English. The entire Listening test will last approximately 45 minutes. There are four parts, and directions are given for each part. You must mark your answers on the separate answer sheet. Do not write your answers in the test book.

PART 1

Directions: For each question in this part, you will hear four statements about a picture in your test book. When you hear the statements, you must select the one statement that best describes what you see in the picture. Then find the number of the question on your answer sheet and mark your answer. The statements will not be printed in your test book and will be spoken only one time.

Sample Answer

Example

 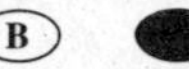 

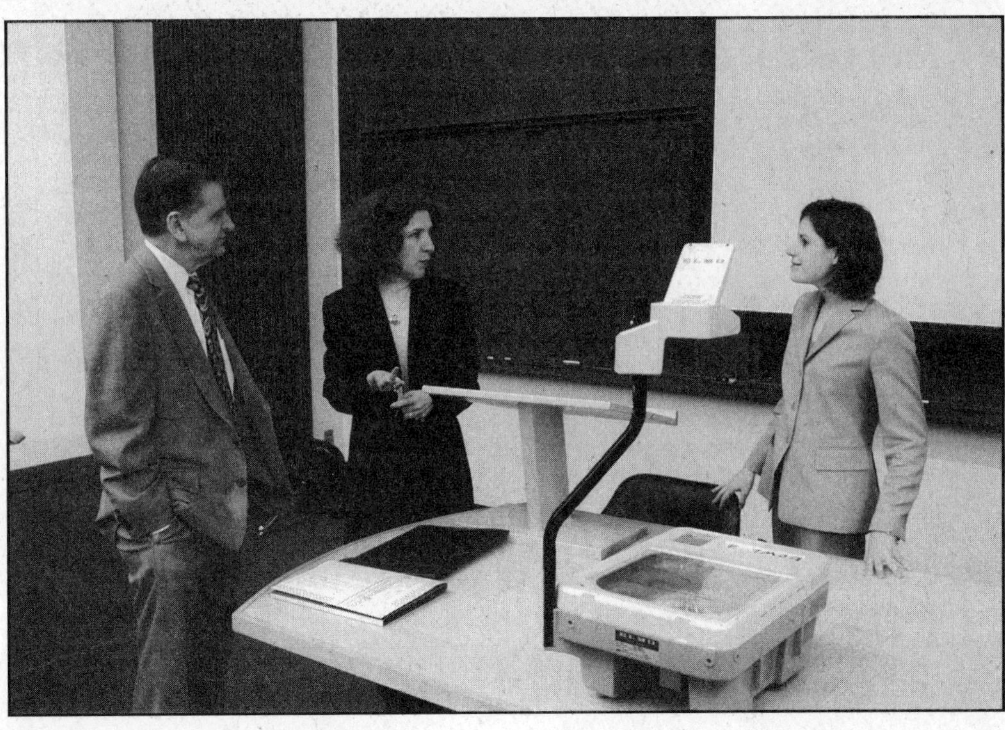

Statement (C), "They're standing near the table," is the best description of the picture, so you should select answer (C) and mark it on your answer sheet.

1.

2.

3. 

4. 

5.

6.

7. 

8. 

9. 

10. 

PART 2

Directions: You will hear a question or statement and three responses spoken in English. They will not be printed in your test book and will be spoken only one time. Select the best response to the question or statement and mark the letter (A), (B), or (C) on your answer sheet.

Sample Answer

(A) ● (C)

Example

You will hear: Where is the meeting room?

You will also hear: (A) To meet the new director.
(B) It's the first room on the right.
(C) Yes, at two o'clock.

Your best response to the question "Where is the meeting room?" is choice (B), "It's the first room on the right," so (B) is the correct answer. You should mark answer (B) on your answer sheet.

11. Mark your answer on your answer sheet.

12. Mark your answer on your answer sheet.

13. Mark your answer on your answer sheet.

14. Mark your answer on your answer sheet.

15. Mark your answer on your answer sheet.

16. Mark your answer on your answer sheet.

17. Mark your answer on your answer sheet.

18. Mark your answer on your answer sheet.

19. Mark your answer on your answer sheet.

20. Mark your answer on your answer sheet.

21. Mark your answer on your answer sheet.

22. Mark your answer on your answer sheet.

23. Mark your answer on your answer sheet.

24. Mark your answer on your answer sheet.

25. Mark your answer on your answer sheet.

26. Mark your answer on your answer sheet.

27. Mark your answer on your answer sheet.

28. Mark your answer on your answer sheet.

29. Mark your answer on your answer sheet.

30. Mark your answer on your answer sheet.

31. Mark your answer on your answer sheet.

32. Mark your answer on your answer sheet.

33. Mark your answer on your answer sheet.

34. Mark your answer on your answer sheet.

35. Mark your answer on your answer sheet.

36. Mark your answer on your answer sheet.

37. Mark your answer on your answer sheet.

38. Mark your answer on your answer sheet.

39. Mark your answer on your answer sheet.

40. Mark your answer on your answer sheet.

GO ON TO THE NEXT PAGE

PART 3

Directions: You will hear some conversations between two people. You will be asked to answer three questions about what the speakers say in each conversation. Select the best response to each question and mark the letter (A), (B), (C), or (D) on your answer sheet. The conversations will not be printed in your test book and will be spoken only one time.

41. What does the man want the woman to do?

(A) Type a letter.
(B) Buy him a sweater.
(C) Have lunch with him.
(D) Work this evening.

42. What is the woman doing now?

(A) Eating lunch.
(B) Leaving for the golf course.
(C) Making copies.
(D) Sending e-mail.

43. Where is the man going?

(A) To a restaurant.
(B) To his room.
(C) To the post office.
(D) To the photocopy store.

---

44. When will the phones be installed?

(A) Monday before noon.
(B) Monday afternoon.
(C) Wednesday before noon.
(D) Wednesday afternoon.

45. Why weren't the phones installed last week?

(A) The equipment was out of order.
(B) They couldn't get an appointment.
(C) The order was placed too late.
(D) They didn't bring the right kind of phone.

46. How long have they been waiting for the phones?

(A) Under a week.
(B) One week.
(C) One month.
(D) More than a month.

---

47. How many dozen pens is the man ordering?

(A) Two.
(B) Four.
(C) Six.
(D) Twelve.

48. What colors does he want?

(A) Green and purple.
(B) Green and red.
(C) Red, black, and blue.
(D) Red, black, and purple.

49. How will he pay for the pens?

(A) He will pay by check.
(B) He will pay with cash.
(C) The woman will send him a bill.
(D) The woman will charge it to his account.

---

50. Where does this conversation take place?

(A) At the dinner table.
(B) In a grocery store.
(C) In a bookstore.
(D) At a bakery.

51. What does the man want the woman to do?

(A) Cook a meal.
(B) Stop coughing.
(C) Eat some more.
(D) Sing a song.

52. What does the woman want to do?

(A) Read a book.
(B) Bake a cake.
(C) Drink coffee.
(D) Pick up her mail.

---

53. Who is giving advice?

(A) A travel agent.
(B) A physician.
(C) A teacher.
(D) A golfer.

54. What is the woman's problem?

(A) She lost her job.
(B) She works too much.
(C) She never takes a walk.
(D) She can't decide on a place for a vacation.

55. What will the woman do?

(A) Go to the health club.
(B) Learn to play golf.
(C) Take a vacation.
(D) Hire someone to help her.

---

56. What don't the speakers like?

(A) Spring.
(B) The heat.
(C) The rain.
(D) Standing.

57. How is the weather today?

(A) Sunny.
(B) Cool.
(C) Humid.
(D) Icy.

58. When does this conversation take place?

(A) May.
(B) September.
(C) November.
(D) December.

---

59. What is the man looking for?

(A) His raincoat.
(B) His boots and umbrella.
(C) His bus ticket.
(D) His watch.

60. What is the weather like?

(A) Hot.
(B) Cold.
(C) Rainy.
(D) Misty.

61. When will the bus leave?

(A) In 15 minutes.
(B) In 20 minutes.
(C) In 29 minutes.
(D) In 50 minutes.

---

62. Where does the man live?

(A) By the school.
(B) By the police station.
(C) On a mountain.
(D) Near a pool.

63. How does the woman get to work?

(A) On foot.
(B) By train.
(C) By car.
(D) By bus.

64. What time will the woman meet the man tomorrow?

(A) At 7:00.
(B) At 7:30.
(C) At 11:00.
(D) At 11:30.

GO ON TO THE NEXT PAGE

65. Why didn't the woman read this morning's paper?

(A) She didn't have money to buy one.
(B) She didn't have time to buy one.
(C) It wasn't delivered on time.
(D) She read yesterday's instead.

66. What does the man suggest that the woman do?

(A) Buy a newspaper at the newsstand.
(B) Hear the news on the radio.
(C) Borrow his newspaper.
(D) Read the news on the Internet.

67. What does the man want to do?

(A) Read the woman a story.
(B) Tell the woman about the news.
(C) Buy a newspaper.
(D) Write an article.

---

68. What time did the woman go to bed?

(A) At 7:00.
(B) After 7:00.
(C) At 11:00.
(D) After 11:00.

69. How many hours of sleep does the woman usually get?

(A) Four.
(B) Five.
(C) Eight.
(D) Ten.

70. Why did she get up early?

(A) To do some work.
(B) To work out at the gym.
(C) To finish reading a book.
(D) To get ready for a trip.

PART 4

Directions: You will hear some talks given by a single speaker. You will be asked to answer three questions about what the speaker says in each talk. Select the best response to each question and mark the letter (A), (B), (C), or (D) on your answer sheet. The talks will not be printed in your test book and will be spoken only one time.

71. What is being sold?

(A) Office space.
(B) Office supplies.
(C) Down pillows.
(D) Sailboats.

72. How long does this sale last?

(A) One day.
(B) Three days.
(C) One week.
(D) Eight days.

73. When does the sale end?

(A) Thursday.
(B) Friday.
(C) Saturday.
(D) Sunday.

---

74. What was the weather yesterday?

(A) Rainy.
(B) Foggy.
(C) Sunny.
(D) Clear.

75. When might it snow?

(A) This evening.
(B) Tomorrow morning.
(C) Tomorrow evening.
(D) This weekend.

76. What will the weekend temperature be?

(A) Below freezing.
(B) Right around freezing.
(C) Around 7 degrees Celsius.
(D) About 11 degrees Celsius.

---

77. What kind of news item is this?

(A) An analysis.
(B) A review.
(C) A correction.
(D) A warning.

78. When might this announcement be heard?

(A) Spring.
(B) Summer.
(C) Fall.
(D) Winter.

79. What causes power failure?

(A) Excessive use.
(B) Lack of demand.
(C) Increased supply.
(D) Poor quality fans.

---

80. Who is probably listening to this announcement?

(A) Ticket agents.
(B) Telephone line technicians.
(C) Airline representatives.
(D) Potential travelers.

81. Why is there a delay?

(A) All the agents are busy.
(B) All flights are late.
(C) The fares are going up.
(D) Representatives are on strike.

82. When should travelers to other countries get to the airport?

(A) Two hours before their flight leaves.
(B) Three hours before their flight leaves.
(C) Four hours before their flight leaves.
(D) Five hours before their flight leaves.

GO ON TO THE NEXT PAGE

83. What kind of people are attending the seminar?

(A) Teachers.
(B) Managers.
(C) Waiters.
(D) Gardeners.

84. Which of the following describes Mr. Margalis?

(A) Inexperienced.
(B) Retired.
(C) Speechless.
(D) Young.

85. Where is the announcement being heard?

(A) In a garden.
(B) In a private office.
(C) In a dining hall.
(D) On a train.

---

86. What is needed to enter?

(A) A special pass.
(B) An authorized signature.
(C) A secure vehicle.
(D) A hunting license.

87. Where can passes be obtained?

(A) Within the secure area.
(B) From authorized personnel.
(C) At the Security Office.
(D) At the License Bureau.

88. What should visitors do when leaving the area?

(A) Sign out.
(B) Pay an exit fee.
(C) Give the pass back.
(D) Keep the pass for future visits.

---

89. What kind of work is advertised?

(A) Full-time.
(B) Part-time.
(C) Overtime.
(D) Volunteer.

90. What qualifications are required?

(A) Law degree.
(B) Medical diploma.
(C) Advertising experience.
(D) Office skills.

91. What are job seekers required to do?

(A) Take a test.
(B) Be available immediately.
(C) Fill out an application form.
(D) Understand employment law.

---

92. What time is the report being presented?

(A) At 8:00.
(B) At 10:00.
(C) At 12:00.
(D) At 2:00.

93. What advice is given?

(A) Wear a hat.
(B) Go to bed early.
(C) Have a nice day.
(D) Take your umbrella.

94. What is the weather now?

(A) Rainy.
(B) Clear skies.
(C) Dark clouds.
(D) Windy.

---

95. What kind of place is Family Security Systems?

(A) A police station.
(B) A travel agency.
(C) An insurance company.
(D) An alarm installation company.

96. For urgent problems, what number should be pressed?

(A) 1.
(B) 4.
(C) 5.
(D) 6.

97. How can you register an address change?

(A) Press 4.
(B) Visit the website.
(C) Speak to an agent.
(D) Send it in by mail.

---

98. Where is this announcement made?

(A) At a school.
(B) At an airport.
(C) At a grocery store.
(D) At a shopping mall.

99. What is today's special?

(A) Chicken.
(B) Beef.
(C) Spaghetti.
(D) Vegetables.

100. What do kids get with their meal?

(A) A toy.
(B) Free dessert.
(C) Extra vegetables.
(D) A seat by the entrance.

This is the end of the Listening test. Turn to Part 5 in your test book.

READING TEST

In the Reading test, you will read a variety of texts and answer several different types of reading comprehension questions. The entire Reading test will last 75 minutes. There are three parts, and directions are given for each part. You are encouraged to answer as many questions as possible within the time allowed.

You must mark your answers on the separate answer sheet. Do not write your answers in the test book.

PART 5

Directions: A word or phrase is missing in each of the sentences below. Four answer choices are given below each sentence. Select the best answer to complete the sentence. Then mark the letter (A), (B), (C), or (D) on your answer sheet.

101. Both companies are __________ the same business.

(A) in
(B) with
(C) from
(D) through

102. __________ there were so many options, everyone was satisfied.

(A) If
(B) Why
(C) Because
(D) When

103. If they __________ more aware of the trends, they could have avoided bankruptcy.

(A) were
(B) are
(C) have been
(D) had been

104. Make checks __________ to the company.

(A) paid
(B) payable
(C) paying
(D) pay

105. Ms. Bolton is both a strong manager __________ a skilled negotiator.

(A) or
(B) with
(C) and
(D) though

106. __________ the stockbrokers said the market was healthy, they refused to invest more money.

(A) Because
(B) Although
(C) In addition
(D) So

107. The seminar will adjourn __________ five o'clock.

(A) in
(B) on
(C) at
(D) the

108. Marketing is important; __________, we're hiring a new public relations firm.

(A) therefore
(B) even though
(C) nevertheless
(D) but

109. The secretary had the messenger __________ the envelope as soon as possible.

(A) delivering
(B) to deliver
(C) deliver
(D) delivered

110. The board meetings usually __________ on time.

(A) have started
(B) start
(C) are starting
(D) have been starting

111. Everyone was disappointed to hear that the company's proposal was __________.

(A) turned up
(B) turned on
(C) turned away
(D) turned down

112. Even though the exchange rate was high, we __________ from them.

(A) buy
(B) must have bought
(C) had to buy
(D) had better buy

113. __________ Dr. Rossi hired the new assistant, the office has become more organized.

(A) When
(B) Before
(C) While
(D) Since

114. Mr. Cutler will __________ as president.

(A) step out
(B) step down
(C) step from
(D) step through

115. Ms. Silva sent the memo __________ it had been approved.

(A) so
(B) but
(C) after
(D) until

116. It's time to take advantage of current __________ rates.

(A) interesting
(B) interest
(C) interested
(D) interests

117. The manager has to __________ the presentation until next week.

(A) put off
(B) put with
(C) put on
(D) put through

118. When the directors __________ a profit, they'll be satisfied.

(A) will see
(B) are seeing
(C) see
(D) have been seeing

119. Do __________ an estimate before getting it in writing.

(A) not ever accept
(B) never accept
(C) accept never
(D) not accept ever

120. The shipment of the new office furniture was __________, so it arrived a week later than expected.

(A) damaged
(B) delayed
(C) repaired
(D) accounted

121. The distributors will collaborate __________ a British company.

(A) with
(B) in
(C) from
(D) of

122. If banks __________ the number of credit cards, the economy would improve.

(A) limiting
(B) limited
(C) had limited
(D) are limiting

GO ON TO THE NEXT PAGE

123. We will need to get the key from the building superintendent so that we can __________ the conference room over the weekend.

(A) access
(B) assist
(C) apply
(D) attend

124. The host will want the total amount __________ before paying the bill.

(A) checked
(B) be checked
(C) checking
(D) check

125. The new sales manager cooperates with her colleagues; __________, she is a valued member.

(A) although
(B) however
(C) for example
(D) therefore

126. __________ our office, Mr. James voted against the proposal.

(A) Representation
(B) Representative
(C) Representing
(D) Representative of

127. You need to __________ your supervisor as soon as possible if you see that a deadline will not be met.

(A) report
(B) permit
(C) inform
(D) converse

128. There has been a decline in local __________ national advertising.

(A) therefore
(B) so
(C) but
(D) and

129. Mr. Kim will have a chance to review all the documents during his __________ with his lawyer next week.

(A) appointment
(B) calendar
(C) agenda
(D) schedule

130. The CEOs will meet __________ Chicago next month.

(A) at
(B) in
(C) to
(D) from

131. The award was contested by one of the __________.

(A) competitors
(B) competition
(C) competing
(D) competitive

132. We will need to work more __________ if we want to get this report finished by the deadline.

(A) slowly
(B) leisurely
(C) efficiently
(D) intermittently

133. Mr. Wong once lived __________ New Orleans.

(A) in
(B) at
(C) from
(D) on

134. The report focused on the __________ of the study.

(A) foundlings
(B) finds
(C) findings
(D) found

135. The staff __________ the office had been burglarized.

(A) suspicion
(B) suspense
(C) suspicious
(D) suspected

136. __________ all the references to verify the information.

(A) Look by
(B) Look out
(C) Look up
(D) Look to

137. Mary is __________ an excellent writer.

(A) considerate
(B) considered
(C) considerable
(D) considers

138. They __________ the launch of their new company only a year ago.

(A) announce
(B) are announcing
(C) have announced
(D) announced

139. After re-evaluating the proposal, the agency __________ the contract to us.

(A) awarding
(B) had awarded
(C) awarded
(D) awards

140. My supervisor had me __________ the morning taking inventory.

(A) spend
(B) to spend
(C) spent
(D) spending

GO ON TO THE NEXT PAGE

PART 6

Directions: Read the texts that follow. A word or phrase is missing in some of the sentences. Four answer choices are given below each of the sentences. Select the best answer to complete the text. Then mark the letter (A), (B), (C), or (D) on your answer sheet.

Questions 141–143 refer to the following letter.

Chandi Akella
Rapid Technology, Inc.
450 Cherry Circle
Detroit, MI 40355

Dear Ms. Akella:

I was interested to read about your company in the online issue of "Technology Today." Perhaps your company's technology can help us.

I own a candy company in Tennessee. We _________ a variety of kinds

141. (A) consume
(B) manufacture
(C) purchase
(D) desire

of candy which are sold all over the USA and in other countries as well. As part of their work, my employees use heavy equipment and move large boxes every day. Sometimes they fall or hurt their backs. As a result, they _________ days of work. Everyone suffers from this situation.

142. (A) avoid
(B) gain
(C) miss
(D) save

These accidents cost my company a lot of money, and my employees suffer from health problems.

Rapid Technology's "cobots" may help. I understand that a "cobot" is like a robot. However, it is a robot that collaborates—or works with—people. So, you call it a "cobot." Is that correct? I understand that people are _________ when they work with cobots. However, the article I read only

143. (A) safer
(B) more safely
(C) safety
(D) more safety

discussed cobots at car companies. Could they also be used at a candy company?

We are very interested in cobots, but we are not sure if they would work here. What do you think? Please reply via mail. Thank you.

Best wishes,

Priscilla Parton

Priscilla Parton
President, Prissy's Candies

GO ON TO THE NEXT PAGE

Questions 144–146 refer to the following e-mail.

To: All Personnel
From: Marcella Fink, Human Resources Office
Subject: Professional Development Opportunities

We have been working hard to put together a variety of professional development opportunities for the coming year. The schedule of company-sponsored workshops and seminars is now ready. We have posted __________ on the company website,

144. (A) them
(B) her
(C) his
(D) it

where it is accessible to all. We have decided against distributing hard copies of the schedule as photocopying is very __________ and our budget is limited. The first

145. (A) costly
(B) useful
(C) necessary
(D) common

workshop of the year, *Effective Use of Spreadsheets*, will take place on January 23. There are only a certain number of spaces available, and we ask anyone interested in attending to sign __________ by the end of this week. Please notify me by e-mail

146. (A) in
(B) up
(C) out
(D) over

if you would like to attend, and I will add your name to the list. Thank you.

Questions 147–149 refer to the following letter.

RDA COMPANY
5943 Alton Lane
Irvine, CA 91628

Office Services, Incorporated
Ms. Misato Sakai
1300 Lincoln Lane
San Francisco, CA 94043

Dear Ms. Sakai:

My boss recommended your company as the fastest at shipping office supplies. I work at RDA Company, and we urgently need some supplies. I hope that you can ship these items ________.

147. (A) quickly
(B) quicker
(C) quickest
(D) quickness

We need two large desks, model 156A, one dark brown and the other black. We also need two chairs for the new desks. We would like the colors to ________ the desks, so please send one dark brown and one black chair.

148. (A) contrast with
(B) differ from
(C) match
(D) cover

We need one new computer, model ABG439, with a medium-sized, flat-screen monitor. Please ________ two speakers.

149. (A) include
(B) included
(C) to include
(D) will include

We also need ten boxes of white, letter-sized paper.

Please send everything immediately. Our new employees need these supplies as soon as possible. Thank you for your assistance.

Regards,

Naser Abdelwali

Naser Abdelwali
Human Resources Director

GO ON TO THE NEXT PAGE

Questions 150–152 refer to the following letter.

The Little Tea Room
Blumberg 77
Adlkofen, Germany

Dr. Johannes Spieker
Hinterkirchstrasse 15
Frieburg, Germany

January 7, 20__

Dear Dr. Spieker:

I wanted to write and personally thank you for your kind effort in helping to tend to one of our ________ at our restaurant in her time of need. Briana

150. (A) doctors
(B) nurses
(C) customers
(D) employees

Hilton, the woman you helped resuscitate on Monday, gave me your name and address when I spoke to her on the phone today. You ________ be glad to

151. (A) had better
(B) could
(C) will
(D) are

know that she is recovering in the hospital and is almost ready to be released.

As it turns out, you assumed correctly that the woman was suffering from a severe and sudden allergic reaction to nuts. She had neglected to inform the waitress that she couldn't eat any food containing nuts. Your skill and presence of mind saved her from suffering a terrible tragedy.

Please bring your family in for a complimentary meal at your earliest convenience so ________ I may thank you in person.

152. (A) that
(B) thus
(C) there
(D) this

Sincerely,

Henrik Andresen

Henrik Andresen, Manager

PART 7

Directions: In this part you will read a selection of texts, such as magazine and newspaper articles, letters, and advertisements. Each text is followed by several questions. Select the best answer for each question and mark the letter (A), (B), (C), or (D) on your answer sheet.

Questions 153–154 refer to the following job announcement.

> **SALES**
>
> California-based company seeking to expand its sales overseas is looking for sales professionals to cover territory in the Pacific Rim region. Successful candidates will have a minimum of two years' experience in sales, preferably in the clothing industry, as well as a good professional appearance, excellent communication skills, and a college degree. Conversational knowledge of Japanese or Mandarin Chinese and experience traveling or working in Asia are desirable. Job is based in San Francisco but requires one to two weeks a month of travel. We offer an excellent salary and benefits package including health and life insurance, relocation allowance, and professional development opportunities. Send résumé and two letters of reference to: J. M. Schmidt, 150 State Street, San Francisco, CA 94181. Closing date: June 15.

153. Who would most likely apply for this job?

(A) An engineer
(B) A real estate agent
(C) A professor
(D) A clerk in a clothing store

154. Which of the following is NOT mentioned as a requirement?

(A) Good appearance
(B) Previous experience
(C) A master's degree
(D) Good speaking and writing skills

Questions 155–157 refer to the following article.

> These days, everybody buys computer software. Consumers purchase all kinds of software, from games for the kids to highly sophisticated professional programs and everything in between. Computer software has become part of everybody's daily life, and this is just one more thing adding to an ever-growing problem. The excessive packaging on computer software is joining catchy wrappers, durable plastic and cardboard boxes, plastic jugs, and other types of packaging in the trash. Everything we buy is packaged in one way or another. When we get our purchases home, we unwrap them and throw the packaging in the trash. It then ends up in the nation's garbage dumps. Communities all around the country are struggling with the problem of where to put all this waste. Much of this excessive packaging serves only to make the products more attractive to consumers. It catches the eye but does not really protect the goods from damage. Environmentalists are asking consumers to say "No!" to wasteful packaging practices. Please purchase only those products that come with a minimum of packaging or that are packaged in 100% recycled materials.

155. What is this article about?

(A) Recycling
(B) Computer software
(C) The use of garbage dumps
(D) A problem with packaging

156. According to the passage, why are products packaged?

(A) For protection
(B) For attractiveness
(C) For ease of consumption
(D) For environmental safety

157. What happens to most packaging?

(A) It's recycled.
(B) It's discarded.
(C) It's stored on shelves.
(D) It's redesigned.

Questions 158–160 refer to the following table.

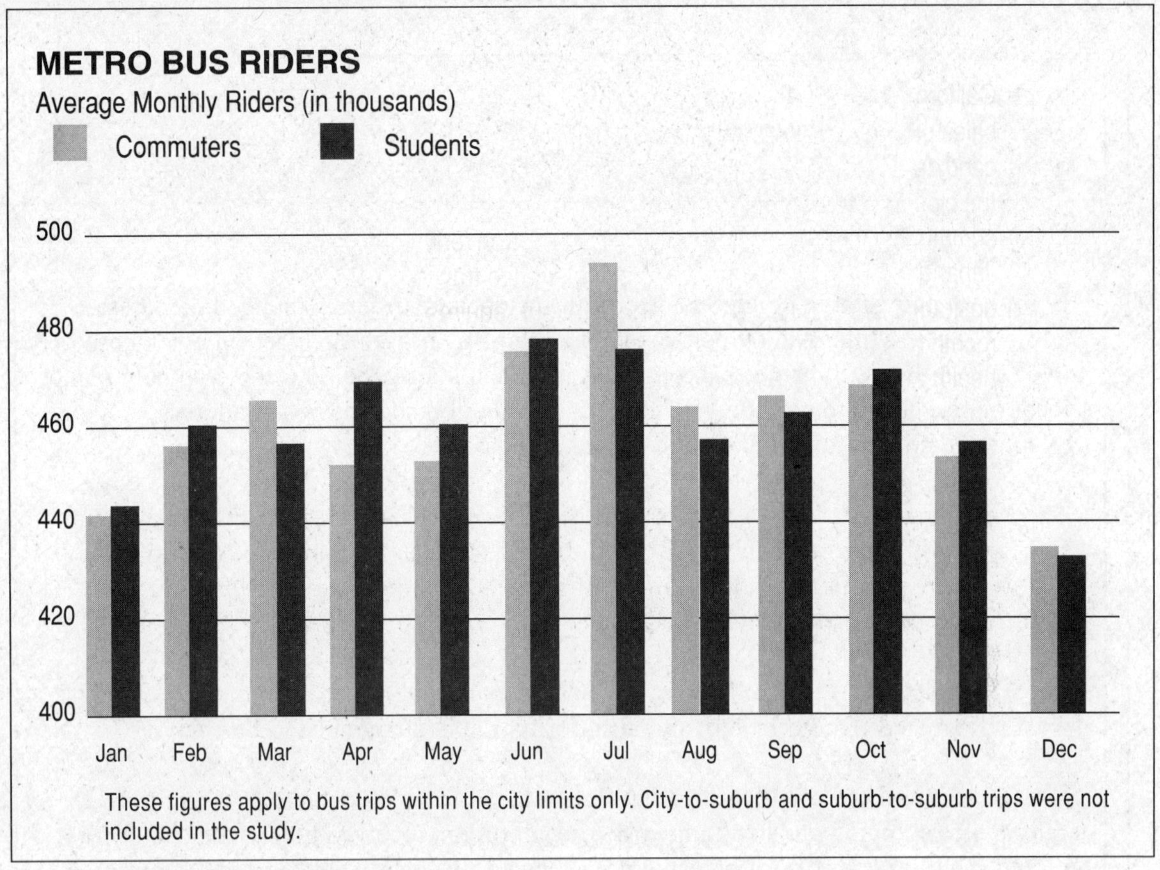

158. What does this table compare?

(A) Daily schedules
(B) Means of transportation
(C) Monthly ridership
(D) Riders with drivers

159. Which month had the highest number of commuters?

(A) June
(B) July
(C) September
(D) October

160. In which month were the buses used least?

(A) February
(B) May
(C) August
(D) December

GO ON TO THE NEXT PAGE

Questions 161–164 refer to the following e-mail.

From: Lars Andersen
To: undisclosed recipients
Subject: directory

Dear Business Owner:

If you are interested in doing business with European partners, you need the latest edition of The Millennial Directory of European Businesses, an electronic database of over one million companies based in Europe. Each listing includes the company name, location, description, website, and contact information such as postal address, telephone number, fax number, and e-mail address.

The Millennial Directory of European Businesses places all this information at your fingertips with its wide menu of search options as well as an option for unlimited export of any data in a variety of different formats, making it a breeze to add this information to your own databases.

The Millennial Directory of European Businesses has been updated annually since it was first created five years ago, and all information is guaranteed to be accurate.

The Millennial Directory of European Businesses is available at the low price of 325 Euros, plus shipping and handling costs, for all orders received before the end of this month. That's 25 Euros off the usual price. Please visit our website to place your order: www.eurobusdirect.com.

Thank you for your interest.

Lars Andersen
The Millennial Directory of European Businesses, Ltd

161. Who would be most interested in this information?

(A) A business owner
(B) A database expert
(C) An editor
(D) A website developer

162. How often is the directory updated?

(A) Every month
(B) Twice a year
(C) Every year
(D) Every five years

163. The word "accurate" in paragraph 3, line 2, is closest in meaning to

(A) interesting
(B) useful
(C) complete
(D) correct

164. What is the usual price of the directory?

(A) 25 Euros
(B) 300 Euros
(C) 325 Euros
(D) 350 Euros

Questions 165–168 refer to the following information.

1. The One-Call System

In most states, natural gas industry–supported laws require contractors and private landowners to call the local One-Call number before beginning any kind of digging. With forty-eight hours' notice, a pipeline operator will locate the pipeline and mark it clearly. Any damage at all to a pipe—even the slightest scratch—could lead to a leak later on. Whether One-Call has become the law in your state or not, you can help keep pipelines safe by calling the number on the right-of-way markers before you dig.

2. Leak Detection

Most pipelines are operated twenty-four hours a day from a control station, using telephone, satellite, or microwave communications systems. Computers are widely used to monitor conditions along the line every ten to sixty seconds, sounding an alarm if they detect any abnormality or sudden change in pressure. In the event of an alarm, valves can be closed and nearby pipeline crews dispatched within minutes.

3. Emergency Response Preparedness

Although leaks occur infrequently and rarely result in a fire, readiness for any emergency is a crucial responsibility for pipeline companies. Federal and state laws supported by the natural gas industry require pipeline companies and local police and fire departments to maintain a coordinated plan of response and to practice for an emergency by staging drills. These drills and personnel training programs emphasize the need for immediate action and for cooperation between the various rescue agencies and the pipeline company.

4. Public Awareness

The One-Call system, state-of-the-art leak detection equipment, and emergency response procedures have all been put in place with one thing in mind—the safety of you, the public. Please visit the website of the Natural Gas Association to find out more about our safety procedures, tips for using natural gas safely in your home, and information on what to do if you see someone tampering with pipeline right-of-way markers.

165. What is the main focus of this passage?

(A) Safety
(B) Personnel training
(C) Computer monitoring
(D) Industry-supported laws

166. What is One-Call?

(A) A telecommunications firm
(B) An excavating company
(C) A contractor
(D) A pipeline detection safety service

167. What do rescue agencies and pipeline companies coordinate?

(A) Leaks
(B) Drilling
(C) Emergency readiness
(D) Microwave communications

168. The word "dispatched" in paragraph 2, line 4, is closest in meaning to

(A) fired
(B) fixed
(C) sent
(D) hired

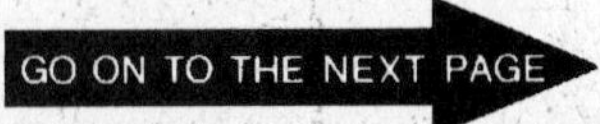

Questions 169–171 refer to the following manual.

TROUBLESHOOTING

If your TV does not work, check the following points:

PICTURE	SOUND	POSSIBLE CAUSES	WHAT TO DO
No picture	Noise	Not properly tuned	Adjust tuning
Picture visible	No sound	• Volume control dial turned too low • Earphones inserted	• Turn up volume • Disconnect earphones
Picture all white	Sound heard	Brightness control not set correctly	Adjust brightness control
Picture dark or blurred	Sound heard	Brightness control not set correctly	Adjust brightness control

169. What is this chart used for?

(A) To determine a problem with a TV
(B) To pick a TV program
(C) To compare prices
(D) To wrap packages

170. What does the manual advise if the picture is all white?

(A) Turn down the volume
(B) Adjust the brightness control
(C) Adjust the tuning
(D) Disconnect the earphones

171. When should the tuning be adjusted?

(A) When there is no picture and no sound
(B) When there is a picture but no sound
(C) When the picture is white
(D) When there is noise but no picture

Questions 172–174 refer to the following letter.

April 23, 20__

China Books, Inc.
23405 San Antonio Ave.
San Fernando, CA 94509

To whom it may concern:

I have just received a "Payment Due" notice from your office. This is the second time I have received such a notice. I don't understand why I have received these notices since I paid for my purchase at the time I placed my order. I enclosed a check in the envelope with the order form. The first time I received a notice, I sent you a photocopy of the canceled check as proof of payment. I am now enclosing, for the second time, a photocopy of both sides of canceled check #535 in the amount of $35.95, which I sent to cover payment for the book *In a Modern World*, plus shipping and handling costs. Please note that the date on the check is October 13. The information on the back shows that it was endorsed and deposited into your company's bank account on October 23.

Please call me at (415) 555-4856 to acknowledge receipt of this letter. I wish to avoid any further harassment about this payment. Your company is a wonderful source for hard-to-find books about Asia, and I would like to continue doing business with you. As a professor of Asian Studies, I am a frequent buyer of books dealing with all aspects of Asian culture and history and often recommend your store to my students. However, if we cannot resolve this matter quickly, I will have to take my business elsewhere. I sincerely hope that will not be necessary.

Sincerely,

Margaret Tomkins

Margaret Tomkins

172. Who owes money?

(A) No one
(B) Ms. Tomkins
(C) China Books
(D) The author

173. When was the check written?

(A) April 23
(B) May 30
(C) October 13
(D) October 23

174. According to the letter, which of the following is NOT true?

(A) Ms. Tomkins has paid twice.
(B) This is Ms. Tomkins' second letter.
(C) Ms. Tomkins has received two notices.
(D) The company received the payment.

Questions 175–176 refer to the following report.

When personal computers first began showing up in offices around the world, people believed that this business tool would lead to something called the "paperless office." This was hailed as a great advance in business practices.

The "paperless office" theory went something like this: people would store their information on disks and computers instead of using file folders and paper. As a result, paper use would decrease. This was supposed to help preserve natural resources as well as reduce the world's solid-waste disposal problem.

In some ways this theory has played out in practice. In offices everywhere around the world, files and records are increasingly being stored electronically rather than on paper. But the prediction has not proven to be entirely true. Documents are often printed out in part or in their entirety in order to be reviewed or shared with others. Often multiple versions of a document go through the printout stage, thus actually increasing the use of paper for each document rather than reducing it. In addition, computers have made it easier to generate notices and flyers, of which people readily make multiple copies to distribute to as wide an audience as possible. In some ways, computers have made it easier than ever before to use large quantities of paper.

So, while computers have reduced paper use in some areas, they have increased it in others. The issue of felling forests in order to manufacture paper and the question of how to dispose of so much solid waste still remain problematic.

175. What is the report about?

(A) Selling computers
(B) Desktop publishing
(C) The "paperless office"
(D) World problems

176. What would the "paperless office" have done?

(A) Preserved resources
(B) Confused secretaries
(C) Cut costs
(D) Improved communication

Questions 177–180 refer to the following job announcement.

Public Health
Pakistan

Position Available: Division of Public Health and Clinical Nutrition. The University of Karachi at Karachi General Hospital (KGH) is recruiting for an assistant clinical professor of medicine for the Division of Public Health and Clinical Nutrition. The candidate will participate in all teaching, clinical, and basic research activities of the division and serve as chief of the public health clinic at KGH. The individual will be expected to develop independently funded clinical research programs dealing with basic public health issues and/or clinical nutrition. Board certification required. Competitive salary in U.S. dollars, airfare, and full board/lodging included. Professional growth and cultural opportunities abound. Send curriculum vitae, summary of clinical research interests, and three letters of reference to Faroque Khan, MD, 572 St. Kilda Road, Sydney 2000, Australia.

177. In line 2, the word "recruiting" is closest in meaning to

(A) hiring
(B) training
(C) helping
(D) funding

178. Which of the following is part of the job description?

(A) Giving blood tests
(B) Supervising research
(C) Repairing equipment
(D) Diagnosing patients

179. Which of the following is a requirement for employment?

(A) Pakistani medical license
(B) Medical board certification
(C) Clinical nutrition training experience
(D) Abstracts of published articles

180. Which of the following is NOT necessary to apply?

(A) Curriculum vitae
(B) References
(C) Clinical research summary
(D) Abstracts of published articles

Questions 181–185 refer to the following purchase order and letter.

PURCHASE ORDER
Ship Prepaid—Add all delivery charges on invoice

Fish Market Restaurant
905 North High Street
Baltimore, MD 21002

Tel: (401) 555-5154
Fax: (401) 555-5177

Vendor:
Super Seafood Suppliers
39908 Cold Spring Circle
Baltimore, MD 21117
Tel: (401) 555-0087
Fax: (401) 555-0097

Ship To: Joey Farina
Restaurant Manager
Address above

Reference: Purchase Order 9855
Date: April 9, 20__

Invoice To: Catherine Cox
Accounting Department
Address above

Delivery Date: April 16, 20__

Item	**Number**	**Quantity**	**Unit Cost**	**Total Cost**
Tuna	S8704T	200 pounds	$4.00	$ 800.00
Lobster	S4399L	150 pounds	8.00	1200.00
Shrimp	S3280S	350 pounds	6.00	2100.00
Salmon	S2956A	300 pounds	8.00	2400.00
Subtotal				6500.00
Shipping/Handling 5%				325.00
TOTAL				$6825.00

Prepared by: *Joey Farina*
Date: *April 8, 20__*

CC: Accounting Department; Purchasing Department; Receiving Department

April 11, 20__

Mr. Joey Farina
Restaurant Manager
Fish Market Restaurant
905 North High Street
Baltimore, MD 21002

Dear Mr. Farina:

I received your purchase order yesterday, and I need to go over a few items with you. Please call me as soon as you receive this letter. April 16 is coming soon and I have not been able to reach you to discuss the order. Have you received my voicemail messages? We normally need ten days between receiving a purchase order and filling it. You must pay an express service charge of $100 in order to have the order filled by April 16.

I've checked with our suppliers, and we can provide 300 pounds of shrimp and 250 pounds of salmon at the present time. We will provide the remainder as soon after April 16 as possible.

Finally, a correction needs to be made to the shipping/handling fee on the purchase order. Our usual charge for this is twice as much as you assumed. I'm enclosing a revised bill for you. With the express service charge, the change in quantity of shrimp and salmon, and the recalculated shipping/handling fee, your new total comes out to $6,480.

Please call or e-mail me today so that we can discuss your order.

Sincerely yours,

Sandra James

Sandra James
Sales Manager

181. Where does Joey Farina work?

(A) At a fish market
(B) At a seafood restaurant
(C) At a fish canning factory
(D) At a seafood supply house

182. When does Joey Farina want his order delivered?

(A) April 8
(B) April 9
(C) April 11
(D) April 16

183. How long did it take Joey Farina's letter to reach Sandra James?

(A) 1 day
(B) 2 days
(C) 3 days
(D) 4 days

184. What did Joey Farina forget to include in his purchase order?

(A) A shipping address
(B) An order for shrimp and salmon
(C) An express service charge
(D) A shipping and handling fee

185. What is the usual shipping and handling fee charged by Super Seafood Suppliers?

(A) 2%
(B) 2.5%
(C) 5%
(D) 10%

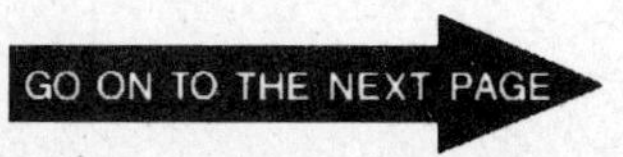

Questions 186–190 refer to the following fax and memo.

FAX COVER SHEET

TECH INTERNATIONAL
Betlemske namesti 11
198 16 Prague
CZECH REPUBLIC
Tel: (204) 12 44
Fax: (204) 12 45

To: All Board Members
From: Jarek Cichy
Marketing Department
Date: November 30, 20__
Pages: This + 5
Ref: Annual Award

Message:

Please review the attached nomination form for our department's nominee for this year's award. Anezka Novotna is my best staff member and is truly deserving of this honor. I am going to Switzerland next week on business and won't return until December 13. I will be checking my e-mail regularly while I'm gone, so please e-mail me if you have any questions about this nominee.

Memo

To: All department staff
From: Jarek Cichy
Re: Annual party—please attend!

As usual, the Board Members are inviting everyone to their annual Appreciation Party held to show their appreciation of the hard work you have all done during the year. This year, as in past years, the Board Members will give out the Employee of the Year award during the party.

I would like to especially encourage each of you to attend the party since this year's Employee of the Year award will be given to the nominee from our department. In addition to the honor and award she will receive from the Board, we're collecting money to buy her a group gift. If everyone contributes just $10, we can buy her the portable DVD player that she wants. See my assistant, Basia, by Thursday at 4:00 to contribute to the gift. I hope to see you all on December 14 at 5:00 P.M.

186. Why did Jarek Cichy send the fax?

(A) To invite employees to a party
(B) To recommend someone for an award
(C) To inform board members of his trip
(D) To ask for money for a gift

187. When will Jarek Cichy return to the office?

(A) November 3
(B) November 30
(C) December 13
(D) December 14

188. What is the purpose of the party?

(A) To honor all company staff
(B) To give an award
(C) To give out presents
(D) To celebrate the holidays

189. Who will receive an award?

(A) Basia
(B) Jarek Cichy
(C) Anezka Novotna
(D) A board member

190. Where does Basia work?

(A) In Switzerland
(B) On the Board of Directors
(C) In the Marketing Department
(D) In the Accounting Department

GO ON TO THE NEXT PAGE

Questions 191–195 refer to the following advertisement and form.

Join our company!

BANGALORE TECHNOLOGY CENTRE (BTC)

Now hiring!

One of the world's top 5 electronics companies
Located in Bangalore, India

Excellent benefits!
Educational assistance, health coverage, free gym membership, paid vacation!
BTC is a great place to work, but don't just take our word for it. Look at the testimony from some of our employees:

"I've worked here for 3 years and it's wonderful. I will work here forever!"
—Manov, Engineering Department

"BTC is the perfect employer. You should apply today."
—Rupal, Marketing Team

"Everyone on the BTC staff is a real team worker, and your supervisors really care about you. It's like one big family."
—Mohan, Accounting Department

Tel: (80) 91 22932001
Fax: (80) 91 22932011
E-mail: btc@btc.com
http: www.btc.com

To learn more, go to our website and fill out the "Request for Information" form.

Request for Information

Learn more about the company called the "Best Technology Company" by the Organization of Computer Engineers.

☑ YES! Send me information about the excellent opportunities at BTC, including the great benefits for employees.

☑ YES! I would like to have a BTC employee contact me.

Name: Bert Roberts
Job: Electrical Engineer
Address: Gulf Harbour Drive
Auckland, New Zealand

Interested in working in: Engineering Department

Tell us something about yourself.
Highest level of education: Master's degree in electrical engineering
Work Experience: 5 years as an electrical engineer at Servitrix, Ltd., Auckland, 2 years as an engineering assistant at R&J Company, Auckland

When you have completed the form, click here.

191. What kind of business is BTC?

(A) A marketing firm
(B) An accounting firm
(C) A computer retail store
(D) An electronics company

192. Which of the following benefits is NOT offered by BTC?

(A) Help paying for school
(B) Medical insurance
(C) Time off with pay
(D) Life insurance

193. How did Bert Roberts get this form?

(A) He visited a website.
(B) Manov sent it to him.
(C) He wrote to BTC to request it.
(D) He found it in the newspaper.

194. How many years of work experience does Bert Roberts have?

(A) Two
(B) Three
(C) Five
(D) Seven

195. If Bert Roberts accepts a job with BTC, what will he probably have to do?

(A) Get a master's degree
(B) Add his testimony to the company's advertisements
(C) Move to another country
(D) Join a gym

Questions 196–200 refer to the following agenda and e-mail.

International Environmental Protection Group (IEPG)
Meeting & Awards Ceremony
Thursday, August 1, 20__ 7:00 P.M.
Place: Room 1, Sofitel Hotel

AGENDA

1. Welcome	Birsen Aksay
2. Fall projects & plans	Ari Tabaku
3. Introduction of Nominating Committee	Kazadi Koite
4. Presentation of award Recipient: J. S. Choi, CEO	Jakob Skolnik
5. Reception	

To: Jakob Skolnik
From: Victoria Williams
Subject: yesterday's awards ceremony

Mr. Skolnik,

We were all concerned about your sudden illness yesterday and hope that you are feeling better today. I know that you will feel reassured to learn that last night's awards ceremony went very well despite your absence. We had Kazadi Koite lead both items 3 and 4, and I am happy to report that he did an excellent job. The CEO of B. J. Technology accepted the award for "most environmentally friendly company" on his company's behalf and expressed great delight on receiving it. The reception was enjoyed by all. We had reserved the room for only three hours, and some guests stayed until the last possible moment. More guests attended than we expected, so we barely had enough room for everyone. Perhaps we should ask for a bigger room next year. Rooms 2 and 3 are also small, but either room 4 or room 6 would be a good size, I think. Even though the ceremony and reception were a great success, I have several other ideas for improvements for next year's ceremony. We can discuss them when you return to work. Please rest well. We hope to see you healthy and back at work soon.

Victoria

196. Who was scheduled to give the welcome speech?

(A) Birsen Aksay
(B) Ari Tabaku
(C) Kazadi Koite
(D) Jakob Skolnik

197. Who presented the award?

(A) Jakob Skolnik
(B) Victoria Williams
(C) Kazadi Koite
(D) Ari Tabaku

198. In which room was the reception held?

(A) Room 1
(B) Room 2
(C) Room 3
(D) Room 4

199. What time did the reception end?

(A) 3:00
(B) 6:00
(C) 7:00
(D) 10:00

200. What does Victoria Williams suggest doing next year?

(A) Asking Jakob Skolnik to present the award
(B) Using a larger hotel
(C) Inviting more guests
(D) Reserving a different room

Stop! This is the end of the test. If you finish before time is called, you may go back to Parts 5, 6, and 7 and check your work.

Practice Test Two

You will find the Answer Sheet for Practice Test Two on page 169. Detach it from the book and use it to record your answers. Play the audio for Practice Test Two when you are ready to begin.

LISTENING TEST

In the Listening test, you will be asked to demonstrate how well you understand spoken English. The entire Listening test will last approximately 45 minutes. There are four parts, and directions are given for each part. You must mark your answers on the separate answer sheet. Do not write your answers in the test book.

PART 1

Directions: For each question in this part, you will hear four statements about a picture in your test book. When you hear the statements, you must select the one statement that best describes what you see in the picture. Then find the number of the question on your answer sheet and mark your answer. The statements will not be printed in your test book and will be spoken only one time.

Sample Answer

Example

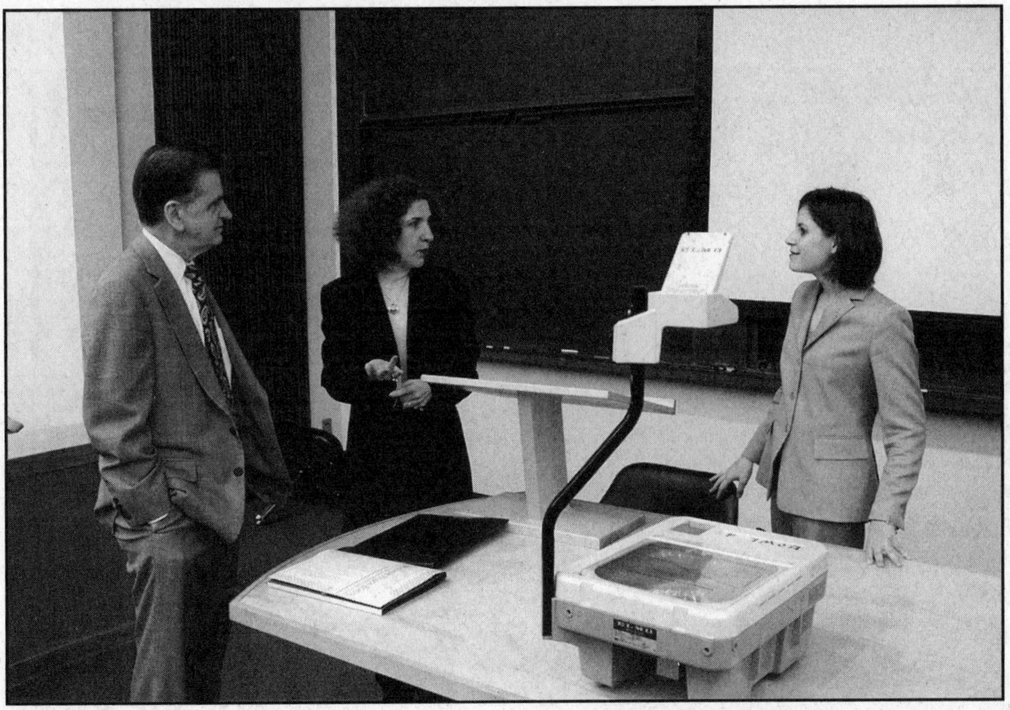

Statement (C), "They're standing near the table," is the best description of the picture, so you should select answer (C) and mark it on your answer sheet.

1.

2.

3.

4.

GO ON TO THE NEXT PAGE

5.

6.

7.

8.

GO ON TO THE NEXT PAGE

9. 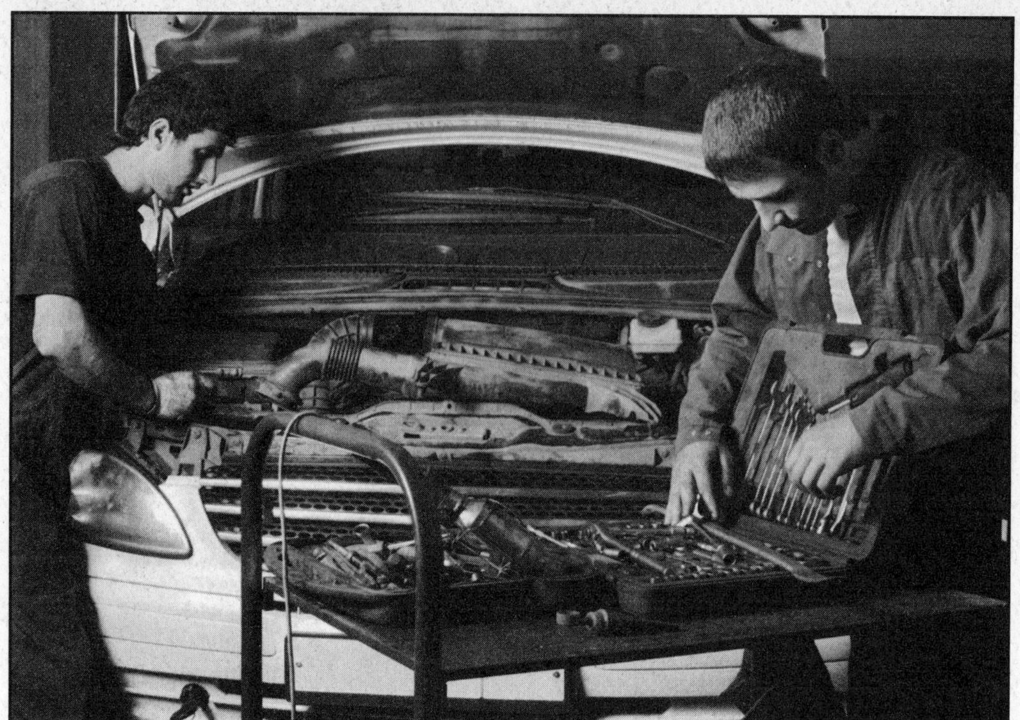

10. 

PART 2

Directions: You will hear a question or statement and three responses spoken in English. They will not be printed in your test book and will be spoken only one time. Select the best response to the question or statement and mark the letter (A), (B), or (C) on your answer sheet.

Sample Answer

Example

You will hear: Where is the meeting room?

You will also hear:
(A) To meet the new director.
(B) It's the first room on the right.
(C) Yes, at two o'clock.

Your best response to the question "Where is the meeting room?" is choice (B), "It's the first room on the right," so (B) is the correct answer. You should mark answer (B) on your answer sheet.

11. Mark your answer on your answer sheet.

12. Mark your answer on your answer sheet.

13. Mark your answer on your answer sheet.

14. Mark your answer on your answer sheet.

15. Mark your answer on your answer sheet.

16. Mark your answer on your answer sheet.

17. Mark your answer on your answer sheet.

18. Mark your answer on your answer sheet.

19. Mark your answer on your answer sheet.

20. Mark your answer on your answer sheet.

21. Mark your answer on your answer sheet.

22. Mark your answer on your answer sheet.

23. Mark your answer on your answer sheet.

24. Mark your answer on your answer sheet.

25. Mark your answer on your answer sheet.

26. Mark your answer on your answer sheet.

27. Mark your answer on your answer sheet.

28. Mark your answer on your answer sheet.

29. Mark your answer on your answer sheet.

30. Mark your answer on your answer sheet.

31. Mark your answer on your answer sheet.

32. Mark your answer on your answer sheet.

33. Mark your answer on your answer sheet.

34. Mark your answer on your answer sheet.

35. Mark your answer on your answer sheet.

36. Mark your answer on your answer sheet.

37. Mark your answer on your answer sheet.

38. Mark your answer on your answer sheet.

39. Mark your answer on your answer sheet.

40. Mark your answer on your answer sheet.

GO ON TO THE NEXT PAGE

PART 3

Directions: You will hear some conversations between two people. You will be asked to answer three questions about what the speakers say in each conversation. Select the best response to each question and mark the letter (A), (B), (C), or (D) on your answer sheet. The conversations will not be printed in your test book and will be spoken only one time.

41. What time will the woman leave?

(A) 4:00.
(B) 5:00.
(C) 5:30.
(D) 7:00.

42. Where will the woman go?

(A) To the train station.
(B) To the airport.
(C) To the office.
(D) To the bus station.

43. What does the man give the woman?

(A) A toothbrush.
(B) A book.
(C) Some newspapers.
(D) Some writing paper.

---

44. How much money does the man need?

(A) Fourteen dollars.
(B) Fifteen dollars.
(C) Forty dollars.
(D) Fifty dollars.

45. What does he need the money for?

(A) To buy lunch.
(B) To pay a sales tax.
(C) To pay his taxi fare.
(D) To buy some reading material.

46. When does the man say he will pay the money back?

(A) This afternoon.
(B) Tomorrow.
(C) The day after tomorrow.
(D) Next week.

---

47. What kind of movie do both speakers like?

(A) Comedies.
(B) War stories.
(C) Murder mysteries.
(D) Westerns.

48. What time does the next movie start?

(A) 4:00.
(B) 7:00.
(C) 7:30.
(D) 10:30.

49. What does the man want to do?

(A) See a war movie.
(B) Stay home.
(C) Watch TV.
(D) Go out.

---

50. When will the meeting be held?

(A) Tuesday.
(B) Wednesday.
(C) Thursday.
(D) Friday.

51. Why has the meeting been postponed?

(A) The accountant is ill.
(B) The room is not ready.
(C) Ms. Schmidt is away at a conference.
(D) The speaker is still reading the budget report.

52. How will people be notified about the postponed meeting?

(A) By phone.
(B) By e-mail.
(C) By letter.
(D) In person.

---

53. Why was the woman late today?

(A) She slept late.
(B) She walked slowly.
(C) She took the bus.
(D) She ran out of gas.

54. How does the man get to work?

(A) By bus.
(B) By car.
(C) On foot.
(D) By train.

55. How long does it take the man to get to work?

(A) 14 minutes.
(B) 35 minutes.
(C) 40 minutes.
(D) 45 minutes.

---

56. Where did the man leave his glasses?

(A) On his desk.
(B) In the woman's office.
(C) In his briefcase.
(D) In the car.

57. What does the woman give the man?

(A) Cash.
(B) Her keys.
(C) A briefcase.
(D) A locket.

58. Where is the woman's car?

(A) In a parking lot.
(B) In front of her office.
(C) Across the street from the park.
(D) In front of the post office.

---

59. What are the speakers talking about?

(A) Eating.
(B) Doing business.
(C) The hot weather.
(D) The city's sidewalks.

60. What does the man sell?

(A) Eggs.
(B) Coolers.
(C) Ice cream.
(D) Air conditioners.

61. Where does the woman work?

(A) At a pool.
(B) At an office.
(C) At a school.
(D) At a restaurant.

---

62. What did the man buy?

(A) A shirt.
(B) A tie.
(C) A suit.
(D) A pair of shoes.

63. Where did he buy it?

(A) In Hong Kong.
(B) At the mall.
(C) Downtown.
(D) At a local department store.

64. What is the woman's opinion of the suit?

(A) It's not very attractive.
(B) It's too expensive.
(C) It's nice-looking.
(D) Its color is great.

GO ON TO THE NEXT PAGE

65. How will the man spend his vacation?

(A) Hiking.
(B) Reading.
(C) Lying in the sun.
(D) Swimming in the sea.

66. How long is his vacation?

(A) Two days.
(B) Eight days.
(C) Two weeks.
(D) Three weeks.

67. When will his vacation begin?

(A) This afternoon.
(B) On Sunday.
(C) On Tuesday.
(D) In a few weeks.

68. How many buses are there?

(A) One.
(B) Two.
(C) Three.
(D) Four.

69. Where will the buses leave from?

(A) The hotel.
(B) The convention center.
(C) The bus station.
(D) The loading dock.

70. How often should the buses leave?

(A) Every five minutes.
(B) Every ten minutes.
(C) Every fifteen minutes.
(D) Every thirty minutes.

PART 4

Directions: You will hear some talks given by a single speaker. You will be asked to answer three questions about what the speaker says in each talk. Select the best response to each question and mark the letter (A), (B), (C), or (D) on your answer sheet. The talks will not be printed in your test book and will be spoken only one time.

71. When will the Revenue Office in City Hall be open?

(A) From 8:00 A.M. to 12:00 on Saturday.
(B) Every day this week.
(C) In the afternoon only.
(D) From 8:00 A.M. to 5:00 P.M., Monday through Friday.

72. What must be filed?

(A) Citizenship papers.
(B) Tax forms.
(C) Time reports.
(D) Housing requests.

73. Why should people come early?

(A) To get a refund.
(B) To become citizens.
(C) To avoid long lines.
(D) To pick up their files.

---

74. Where would this announcement be heard?

(A) At a subway station.
(B) In a hotel.
(C) On an airplane.
(D) At an airport.

75. Which signs should passengers follow for rental cars?

(A) Blue.
(B) Red.
(C) Green.
(D) Yellow.

76. How can passengers get to their cars?

(A) By city bus.
(B) By shuttle.
(C) By subway.
(D) By walking.

---

77. When will the speech be heard?

(A) Before lunch.
(B) After lunch.
(C) Next month.
(D) Next Friday.

78. How often are the luncheons held?

(A) Every Friday.
(B) Every month.
(C) Twice a month.
(D) Once a year.

79. What is Dr. Jenny Chang's profession?

(A) Politician.
(B) Criminal.
(C) Saleswoman.
(D) Author.

---

80. What should employees do if a badge is lost?

(A) Ask the security office for a replacement.
(B) Report to their supervisor.
(C) Request a visitor pass.
(D) Leave the building.

81. How may visitors enter the building?

(A) With an employee escort.
(B) With permission from security personnel.
(C) With an identification badge.
(D) With proper dress.

82. Who must wear identification badges?

(A) All employees.
(B) Potential employees.
(C) Visitors with escorts.
(D) Visitors alone.

GO ON TO THE NEXT PAGE

83. What is opening?

(A) The Civic Center.
(B) A new golf course.
(C) A downtown office.
(D) A residential hotel.

84. What is being offered?

(A) Golf lessons.
(B) City apartments.
(C) New watches.
(D) Club memberships.

85. What is the cost of a one-year membership?

(A) $600.
(B) $650.
(C) $700.
(D) $1,100.

---

86. What is the weather perfect for?

(A) Going to the beach.
(B) Bicycling in the mountains.
(C) Playing golf.
(D) Watching the races.

87. How is the sun described?

(A) Rising.
(B) Hazy.
(C) Shining.
(D) Bright.

88. What will the weather be like on Saturday?

(A) Very hot.
(B) Sunny.
(C) Cloudy.
(D) Rainy.

---

89. How much was the man's estate worth?

(A) Nothing.
(B) Under two thousand dollars.
(C) A million dollars.
(D) Over two million dollars.

90. Who inherited the money?

(A) His children.
(B) His wife.
(C) His dog.
(D) His best friend.

91. When will the funeral be held?

(A) Sunday.
(B) Monday.
(C) Wednesday.
(D) Thursday.

---

92. When is the office open?

(A) Every day of the week.
(B) Only on Monday.
(C) Only on Friday.
(D) Monday through Friday.

93. What service is provided only in the afternoon?

(A) Renewal of driver's licenses.
(B) Applications for new driver's licenses.
(C) Driving tests.
(D) Blood tests.

94. When does the office stop taking customers?

(A) At 12:00.
(B) At 4:00.
(C) At 4:30.
(D) At 5:00.

---

95. What is the caller's complaint?

(A) Her order arrived damaged.
(B) She received something she didn't order.
(C) Her order hasn't arrived yet.
(D) She was charged too much for her order.

96. When did the caller place her order?

(A) One week ago.
(B) Two weeks ago.
(C) Three weeks ago.
(D) Four weeks ago.

97. What does she ask the company to do?

(A) Call her today.
(B) Send her a check.
(C) Deliver the order right away.
(D) Charge the order to her credit card.

---

98. What did CompCo do today?

(A) It hired new employees.
(B) It gave a training workshop.
(C) It negotiated a deal.
(D) It had a celebration.

99. How many employees currently work at CompCo?

(A) 50.
(B) 100.
(C) 150.
(D) 200.

100. What happened when PC Computer Systems closed down?

(A) Many people lost their jobs.
(B) The Intrax Company took its place.
(C) They broke a contract with city leaders.
(D) Other technology businesses left the area.

This is the end of the Listening test. Turn to Part 5 in your test book.

READING TEST

In the Reading test, you will read a variety of texts and answer several different types of reading comprehension questions. The entire Reading test will last 75 minutes. There are three parts, and directions are given for each part. You are encouraged to answer as many questions as possible within the time allowed.

You must mark your answers on the separate answer sheet. Do not write your answers in the test book.

PART 5

Directions: A word or phrase is missing in each of the sentences below. Four answer choices are given below each sentence. Select the best answer to complete the sentence. Then mark the letter (A), (B), (C), or (D) on your answer sheet.

101. Mr. Doh __________ clients' phone calls.

(A) rarely returns
(B) returns rarely
(C) has returned rarely
(D) rarely had returned

102. Success depends __________ the efforts of the organization.

(A) from
(B) in
(C) on
(D) of

103. There has been strong competition; __________, the new company has made great profits.

(A) instead
(B) nonetheless
(C) then
(D) despite

104. Ms. Shirish will resign her position as chief __________ officer.

(A) operator
(B) operational
(C) operation
(D) operating

105. The weather report predicts it will rain __________ become colder.

(A) neither
(B) nor
(C) and
(D) either

106. The printer __________ paper.

(A) ran into
(B) ran out of
(C) ran without
(D) ran over

107. The electricity went out __________ we were making coffee.

(A) so
(B) because of
(C) while
(D) for

108. It is a good idea to __________ your tickets now to make sure you get a seat, but you don't have to pay for them until you pick them up at the box office.

(A) purchase
(B) obtain
(C) reserve
(D) return

109. The sales division reported a 64 percent drop ________ the last sales period.

(A) during
(B) with
(C) at
(D) to

110. ________ the presentation there will be time for questions and answers.

(A) Afterward
(B) Following
(C) End
(D) Finish

111. Get the invoice ________ upon receipt.

(A) signature
(B) sign
(C) signed
(D) signing

112. ________ time to submit a bid.

(A) Still there is
(B) Is there still
(C) There is still
(D) They're still is

113. Our future will be ________ on what services we can provide.

(A) basic
(B) based
(C) basing
(D) base

114. If there ________ better communication, I would not resign.

(A) were
(B) was
(C) is
(D) will be

115. ________ the critics and answer their questions.

(A) Stand in for
(B) Stand at
(C) Stand with
(D) Stand up to

116. By the end of this century, business ________ greatly.

(A) will be changed
(B) will have changed
(C) changes
(D) changed

117. The ________ market has declined in many parts of the country.

(A) homing
(B) housed
(C) homes
(D) housing

118. After ________ for several hours, the directors decided to reject the proposed changes.

(A) referring
(B) inferring
(C) conferring
(D) preferring

119. ________ one partner has resigned, others are quitting, too.

(A) Because
(B) Although
(C) If
(D) Before

120. The management makes an assessment ________.

(A) rarely
(B) still
(C) monthly
(D) already

121. The chairman said his ________ would continue his strategies.

(A) successful
(B) successor
(C) success
(D) successive

122. Mr. Kim was ________ from his job at the accounting firm once it was discovered that he knew very little about accounting.

(A) departed
(B) retreated
(C) advanced
(D) dismissed

GO ON TO THE NEXT PAGE

123. Since 1990, our customers ________ with our service.

(A) are satisfied
(B) have satisfied
(C) have been satisfying
(D) have been satisfied

124. People either don't have the money ________ they aren't willing to spend it.

(A) and
(B) neither
(C) or
(D) although

125. The group is composed ________ five companies.

(A) in
(B) of
(C) up
(D) from

126. In order to make more money, Mr. Garcia has decided to ________ a second job.

(A) take off
(B) take out
(C) take from
(D) take on

127. A survey of the ________ shows they are satisfied with their jobs.

(A) employment
(B) employs
(C) employees
(D) employing

128. ________ the bad location, the management is confident of success.

(A) Despite
(B) Since
(C) With
(D) As

129. Company officials must disclose their own ________ affairs.

(A) finance
(B) financing
(C) financial
(D) financed

130. The new business has ________ incorporated.

(A) still
(B) once
(C) yet
(D) already

131. The road to success ________ of a combination of hard work and good luck.

(A) persists
(B) insists
(C) consists
(D) resists

132. The competitor's attempt to ________ the new company was stopped.

(A) take off
(B) take over
(C) take to
(D) take out

133. The new agent has experience ________ not expertise.

(A) but
(B) and
(C) with
(D) however

134. ________ the flight is canceled, the seminar will have to be postponed.

(A) While
(B) If
(C) Although
(D) Besides

135. The proposal was submitted ________ April 28.

(A) at
(B) the
(C) on
(D) from

136. ________ costs have increased dramatically.

(A) Advertising
(B) Advertisements
(C) Advertised
(D) Advertise

137. Ford Motor Company reported a drop ________ quarterly profits.

(A) to
(B) from
(C) in
(D) with

138. The company was ________ by an immigrant.

(A) found
(B) founding
(C) find
(D) founded

139. Mr. Daley is our most skilled speaker; ________, he is unavailable to give the presentation.

(A) besides
(B) nevertheless
(C) for example
(D) while

140. Have Ms. Alva ________ a press release immediately.

(A) writes
(B) to write
(C) writing
(D) write

GO ON TO THE NEXT PAGE

PART 6

Directions: Read the texts that follow. A word or phrase is missing in some of the sentences. Four answer choices are given below each of the sentences. Select the best answer to complete the text. Then mark the letter (A), (B), (C), or (D) on your answer sheet.

Questions 141–143 refer to the following letter.

Office Works
544 Hudson Street
Boston, MA 34602
Tel: (617) 555-7664 Fax: (617) 555-7670

May 10, 20__

Mary Briddock
Banqueting Director
Wynd's Garden Hotel
219 Center Circle
Boston, MA 03299

Dear Ms. Briddock:

Our company, Office Works, is seeking a place to host a banquet. We will honor our top employees at this event, which will include dinner followed by speeches and the presentation of awards.

At the same time we plan to celebrate an ________ to our

141. (A) addition
(B) additive
(C) addend
(D) addendum

company. We recently purchased the Office Supply Store, and we are now the region's largest seller of office supplies.

We expect approximately 100 guests. We would like to have our event on Saturday, August 15. If no room is available for that date, we could consider ________ it on the following Saturday, August 22.

142. (A) have
(B) to have
(C) having
(D) will have

Could you please mail me your latest price list, descriptive brochure, and menus? I am interested in learning more about ________ facilities and services.

143. (A) my
(B) our
(C) your
(D) their

Thank you.

Lynn Ishii

Lynn Ishii
Events Coordinator

GO ON TO THE NEXT PAGE

Questions 144–146 refer to the following notice.

GLOBAL AIRLINES POLICY STATEMENT

Baggage

Each passenger may carry two items onto the plane: one small suitcase and one personal item. The personal item may be a purse, laptop computer, or briefcase.

The items should fit under the seat in front of you or in the overhead bin. These bins fill quickly, so in case of overload, the flight attendant may place your suitcase in the back of the plane.

In addition ________ the two carry-on items, each passenger may check

144. (A) of
(B) to
(C) with
(D) from

two suitcases to be transported in the airplane's luggage compartment. These suitcases must meet the airline's size limits. ________ baggage

145. (A) Excess
(B) Excelled
(C) Excepted
(D) Executive

charges apply to oversized and additional pieces. These charges must be paid at the time of check-in.

Please ________ a customer service representative if you have questions

146. (A) contact
(B) contacts
(C) to contact
(D) can contact

about this policy.

Questions 147–149 refer to the following magazine article.

Is dentistry the career for you? Today's dentists have many more opportunities than they used to. In the past, a dentist's life was predictable. Most were men who would leave home for a few years to study at a dental school, then return to their hometown, open up an office, and work there their whole life. Most dentists looked forward to this or something similar. Today, dentists are more mobile. Men and women can _________ dental school in

147. (A) will attend
(B) attending
(C) to attend
(D) attend

different places. Some still return to their hometown to work. Others move on to new cities.

Dentists today may specialize in one or more areas. Two common ones are oral surgery and dental public health. Oral surgery focuses _________ treating diseases and problems through

148. (A) in
(B) at
(C) on
(D) to

operations. Dental public health concentrates on improving the dental health of a community. For example, these dentists _________ to schools to teach children how to brush their teeth.

149. (A) go
(B) went
(C) had gone
(D) would go

Some dentists work only in their specialty areas while others do both general and specialty work.

GO ON TO THE NEXT PAGE

Questions 150–152 refer to the following e-mail.

To: frontoffice1
From: geraldinebennett
Re: Doing our part

Dear Mr. Cobalt:

I'm writing to you to express my concern about Pascal's reputation as a wasteful company. I'm sure you read the recent letter to the editor in the *Sydney Daily News* regarding our non-recyclable plastic bottles and caps. Since the letter was printed, ________ have received complaints from

150. (A) we
(B) he and I
(C) they
(D) your

hundreds of customers who are threatening to boycott our company if we don't change our practices. We have also received flyers from ________ manufacturing companies offering to help us become a more

151. (A) varies
(B) variety
(C) various
(D) variable

environmentally friendly company. I have looked briefly into some of these options on my own time but would like to ask your permission to do more.

I would like ________ 20 hours of my upcoming workweek to this cause

152. (A) devote
(B) devoting
(C) to devote
(D) devotion

in hopes of coming up with a viable plan for Pascal's future as a company that cares about recycling. I hope you will agree with me that the health of our natural environment is worth the effort. Please respond as soon as possible.

Sincerely,
Geraldine Bennett, Administrative Assistant
Pascal's Pharmaceuticals

PART 7

Directions: In this part you will read a selection of texts, such as magazine and newspaper articles, letters, and advertisements. Each text is followed by several questions. Select the best answer for each question and mark the letter (A), (B), (C), or (D) on your answer sheet.

GO ON TO THE NEXT PAGE

Questions 153–155 refer to the following fax.

One Devonshire Gardens

7 July, 20__

Fax to: *P. Peterman*
Fax number: *0101-202-555-1218*

Dear Mr. Peterman:

Thank you for your confirmation fax today. We take great pleasure in confirming your reservation of one superior double room for the evenings of 28 through 30 July. The cost of this room will be £135 a night, inclusive of tax, newspaper, and continental breakfast. The total charge of £405 will be made to the credit card number which you previously provided to us.

I would like to take this opportunity to remind you that we have a fully equipped exercise room, as well as an indoor swimming pool, for the exclusive use of our guests at no extra charge. We also have a restaurant located on the premises at which you may purchase lunch or dinner at your discretion.

Should you require transportation from the airport when you arrive in our city, we can arrange a special airport shuttle for you. Just call the hotel from one of the white courtesy phones located throughout the arrivals terminal. Press 15 to reach the One Devonshire Gardens front desk.

We look forward to welcoming you at One Devonshire Gardens. Please don't hesitate to contact me should you have any questions regarding your reservations or our accommodations.

Yours sincerely,

Debbie Smith

Debbie Smith
Reservations Manager

153. What kind of room was reserved?

(A) A single
(B) A twin
(C) A double
(D) A suite

154. Which of the following is NOT included in the price of the room?

(A) Breakfast
(B) Tax
(C) A newspaper
(D) Dinner

155. How did Mr. Peterman make a reservation?

(A) By fax
(B) Through an agent
(C) By letter
(D) In person

Questions 156–159 refer to the following job announcement.

Seeking: Assistant Controller

- Large downtown law firm is seeking an Assistant Controller for our Accounting Department.
- Basic responsibilities include control of the accounting systems, supervision of a seven-person team, and assisting with the hiring and training of new employees.
- Qualified applicant should have eight years of accounting experience, as well as a minimum of two to three years in a supervisory position. Experience working in a law firm is desirable.
- Education requirements include an undergraduate degree in accounting. CPA is preferred.
- The successful candidate will have the necessary computer skills and be familiar with the most current automated financial systems.

To apply for this position, send a résumé and three letters of reference to:
Annabelle Smythe
Forbes, Lawrence, and Ross
187 Oakland Boulevard
Detroit, MI 41084
Closing date: November 12

156. What kind of firm is hiring?

(A) A computer company
(B) An accounting office
(C) An advertising agency
(D) A law firm

157. Which of the following is NOT mentioned as a qualification?

(A) Experience as a supervisor
(B) Familiarity with automated financial systems
(C) A law degree
(D) A degree in accounting

158. What kind of applicant would be most attracted to this job?

(A) A lawyer
(B) An accountant
(C) A computer science major
(D) A director of human resources

159. The word "automated" in paragraph 5, line 2, is closest in meaning to

(A) global
(B) modern
(C) common
(D) mechanical

Questions 160–162 refer to the following letter.

> Dear Customer,
>
> Congratulations! You have just purchased one of the world's most sophisticated microwave ovens. This appliance has been designed with your convenience in mind. It combines an array of special features with ease of use. State-of-the-art features include a temperature sensor so that you will never again have an overcooked or undercooked meal; a 24-hour timer so that you can prepare your food when you have time and have it ready to eat when you are; an automated defrosting system so that you can prepare frozen food with no extra waiting time; a programmable chime system to let you know when your food is ready; and an automatic self-cleaning system so that your oven is always fresh and ready for use.
>
> All of these features and more are available to you at just the push of a button. It is so simple to use. Each feature is completely explained in this manual. Just follow the step-by-step instructions and you will be cooking delicious meals in no time at all! In addition, recipes for various entrees and desserts are included at the back of the manual to get you started on your new adventures in microwave cooking. This product has been designed to give you many years of trouble-free operation as long as the instructions are followed. If for some reason the product should fail, it is completely guaranteed for one year. A complete explanation of the warranty is included on page 15 of the manual. Additional instructions and recipes are available on our website.
>
> Thank you again for becoming a Kitchen Appliances customer.
>
> Sincerely,
>
> *M.S. Fujimoto*
>
> M.S. Fujimoto
> President
> Kitchen Appliances, Inc.

160. Where would this letter most likely be found?

(A) In a microwave manual
(B) In the mail
(C) In an advertisement
(D) In a design store

161. The word "sophisticated" in line 2 is closest in meaning to

(A) popular
(B) advanced
(C) dependable
(D) well-known

162. What can be found on the company's website?

(A) An explanation of the warranty
(B) More instructions and recipes
(C) A Kitchen Appliances price list
(B) M.S. Fujimoto's e-mail address

Questions 163–165 refer to the following press release.

More than 50,000 electronics retailers and distributors are expected at the McCormick Convention Center in Chicago starting next Saturday. Some 1,300 manufacturers from more than 35 countries will exhibit their latest high-technology equipment, including industrial equipment, office machines, and household appliances. The new products won't appear on retailers' shelves until next fall, but show attendees will be able to purchase them during the show at special prices.

Highlights of the show include the following:

- Demonstrations of robots designed for household use. Watch robots perform everyday household chores. Each day, models from a different group of manufacturers will be shown. Hall of Industry, 3:00–5:00 P.M. daily.
- Talks by product developers representing companies from various countries on topics such as *The Impact of Electronic Technology on Business, Future Developments in Technology, How Electronic Technology Will Solve Our Transportation Problems,* and more. Call the Convention Center or visit our website for the speaker list. Wilson Auditorium, 7:00 P.M. nightly.
- Musical equipment demonstrations. Show attendees will be able to try out the latest synthesizers, guitars, and other electronic musical equipment. Exhibit Hall A, ongoing.
- Inventors of Tomorrow, a special hands-on workshop for children ages 10–13. Free with the price of admission to the show, but due to space limitations, pre-registration is required. Call the Convention Center or visit our website to register. Saturday and Sunday, 2:00 P.M.

Visit the Convention Center website for a complete schedule of demonstrations, workshops, and special events going on throughout the show.

Tickets are available by calling the Convention Center or through the Convention Center website. Special prices are available for multi-day passes.

Contact us by phone: 800-555-0913 or on the web.

The Summer Consumer Electronics Show will continue through June 5.

163. What is the main topic of the press release?

(A) The McCormick Convention Center
(B) Chicago's convention centers
(C) Electronics retailers
(D) The Summer Consumer Electronics Show

164. How many manufacturers are expected?

(A) 1,300
(B) 5,000
(C) 13,000
(D) 50,000

165. What is on display at the Convention Center?

(A) High-technology products
(B) Distribution of networks
(C) Retail outlets
(D) Shelving samples

Questions 166–168 refer to the following table.

Programming for Sunday, March 26

	11:30 A.M.
Ch 4	*Business Review* A review of this week's business news. This week's special guest is international business analyst Marilyn Kim of the McGuire Institute.
	1:00 P.M.
Ch 9, 11	*Company Profiles* An in-depth look at significant companies around the world. Featured this week are Limnex, Inc., and Asian Global Industries, two newcomers to the international finance scene.
	1:30 P.M.
Ch 4	*Up Front with Politics and Economics* Discussion of the latest political decisions affecting business and finance. Host Richard Lee interviews political analysts and finance experts.
	2:00 P.M.
Ch 7, 13	*Business Today* Recent innovations in business. This week we visit with Tina and Luis Gomez, who will share how they built their small family clothing business into an international company.
	3:00 P.M.
Ch 4	*World View of Business* News on business around the world, with commentaries by Masafumi Sachimoto and Jacques DeLeon.
	4:00 P.M.
Ch 20	*Making Money* Successful personal investing. This week's topic: "How to Take Advantage of the Real Estate Market." Plus, tips for financing your child's college education.

166. What do these TV listings feature?

(A) Concerts
(B) Business programs
(C) Travelogues
(D) Sports events

167. What begins on TV at 2:00 P.M.?

(A) *Business Today*
(B) *Company Profiles*
(C) *Making Money*
(D) *Business Review*

168. Which station would someone who has money to invest watch?

(A) Ch 4
(B) Ch 7
(C) Ch 11
(D) Ch 20

Questions 169–170 refer to the following announcement.

As a national leader with over forty years of experience providing TV, radio, and marketing services to the corporate world, Abingdon can offer you outstanding career opportunities.

We are looking for energetic, creative, and committed professionals to join the Abingdon family. If you are looking for a position in a dynamic and stimulating work environment with plenty of room for professional growth, we want to talk to you.

We are currently seeking applications for computer programmers and software developers. We offer a competitive salary and benefits, excellent working conditions, and a chance to make a difference.

Please visit our booth at the National Career Center Job Fair during the week of October 13–18 to find out about the exciting job opportunities awaiting you at Abingdon.

* * * * * * * *

169. What type of announcement is this?

(A) A government proclamation
(B) A job announcement
(C) A television listing
(D) Publicity for the opening of a National Career Center

170. Which of the following people would be most interested in this announcement?

(A) A communications major
(B) A retired radio announcer
(C) A production manager
(D) A computer specialist

GO ON TO THE NEXT PAGE

Questions 171–174 refer to the following letter.

International Films, Ltd.
124 West Houston St., New York, NY 10012

July 30, 20__

E. Denikos, Inc.
Earos 42
Aghia Paraskevi 15342
Athens, Greece

Dear Mr. Denikos:

I am writing to you at the request of Ms. Evangelia Makestos, who is applying for a position as an assistant in your company.

Ms. Makestos worked for me as an assistant during her summer vacations for the past three years. My colleagues and I found her to be a very competent and reliable employee. Her duties consisted of typing and copying documents, maintaining files, organizing appointment schedules, assisting visitors to the office, and other office tasks as they arose. She was able to handle multiple tasks and to work independently. She always assisted our clients in a knowledgeable, professional, and patient manner. In addition, she developed a high level of ability in the English language during the time she worked and studied in this country. We had hoped to rehire her at our company in a permanent position when she finished her business course here in New York. However, she has decided to go through with her original plan of returning to Greece.

We will miss Ms. Makestos here at International Films, but I am happy to recommend her as a valuable addition to your company staff. Please feel free to contact me at the above address if you have any questions or need further information.

Sincerely,

Elizabeth Hogan

Elizabeth Hogan, Director
International Films, Ltd.

171. What is Ms. Makestos probably doing?

(A) Job hunting
(B) Quitting her job
(C) Moving to New York
(D) Applying to school

172. The word "competent" in paragraph 2, line 2, is closest in meaning to

(A) responsible
(B) friendly
(C) skilled
(D) useful

173. How long did Ms. Makestos work at International Films?

(A) One summer
(B) Three summers
(C) One year
(D) Three years

174. What kind of letter is this?

(A) A letter of complaint
(B) A job inquiry
(C) A letter of recommendation
(D) A request for information

GO ON TO THE NEXT PAGE

Questions 175–177 refer to the following announcement on the Internet.

Current Issue (#148, March 20–26)
SPP Archive of back issues
Prospects (SPP Culture & Lifestyle Guide)

Moscow DAILY

Subscription Information

To order an international subscription to the English language edition of the *Moscow Daily*, please e-mail Vladimir Alekseev, subscription service manager.

Please include your name and address to receive a subscription coupon.

Yes! I want to subscribe to the ***Moscow Daily*** and have 5 percent of the subscription rate go to the charity of my choice:

Please check one:

- ❑ Protecting Our Natural Resources Organization
- ❑ Clean Oceans Today Association
- ❑ Saving Endangered Species Society

All subscriptions are honored with a money-back guarantee. The first month's issue is complimentary. CONTINUE

- *How to contact us*
- *More about the* Moscow Daily
- *How to subscribe to the printed newspaper*
- *Staff*

Return to Moscow Daily *web home page*

175. What can the reader get by sending an e-mail to Vladimir Alekseev?

(A) A subscription to the *Moscow Daily* in English
(B) An application for employment at the *Moscow Daily*
(C) Information about how to support various charities
(D) A list of newspaper staff members

176. What would happen if the reader were dissatisfied with the newspaper?

(A) The newspaper would send a complimentary issue.
(B) The subscription would be extended.
(C) The reader would be contacted.
(D) The subscription price would be refunded.

177. Which type of charities does the newspaper support?

(A) Disadvantaged children
(B) Disease prevention
(C) Environmental concerns
(D) Art and cultural institutions

Questions 178–180 refer to the following article.

TWO TYPES OF TRAINING

There are two common forms of employee training—on-the-job training and off-the-job training. On-the-job training is the most widely used and least expensive form of training. It consists of an employee learning from a supervisor or co-worker how to do the job. On-the-job training could be described as an apprenticeship. It is efficient because it is done at the workplace while the employee is fulfilling work duties. As time goes by, the employee becomes more and more skilled at the job and eventually can train other employees in turn.

Off-the-job training is the most expensive form of training. It consists of an employee being sent away from the workplace to a training program where training is provided. It is less efficient because it requires the employee to take time away from work duties. In addition, depending on where the training site is located, travel and accommodation expenses may be incurred. And of course, fees must be paid to the person or organization providing the training.

When deciding which form of training to provide, an employer must consider such things as the availability of staff with necessary skills and time to provide on-the-job training and the types of off-site training available, in addition to the expense. It may well be decided that off-the-job training is worth the cost. While the requirements are different for on-the-job training as compared to off-the-job training, the purpose of both types is the same—to improve employee efficiency and productivity.

178. Which of the following best describes on-the-job training?

(A) Expensive
(B) Ineffective
(C) Common
(D) Quick

179. What is on-the-job training similar to?

(A) An apprenticeship
(B) Off-the-job training
(C) A supervisory position
(D) A company benefit

180. According to the passage, what is the purpose of training?

(A) To improve employee efficiency
(B) To spend excess capital
(C) To satisfy government requirements
(D) To please a supervisor

GO ON TO THE NEXT PAGE

Questions 181–185 refer to the following e-mail and directory.

From: Hussein Gitai
To: Olga Montgomery
Subject: Errands for Monday

Olga,

I am out sick today, so there are several errands I'll need you to do for me. I have outlined them below. Please call me at home if this message is not clear.

There are several things to deliver to other floors in the library. All of these items are on my desk, and they must be delivered today. Take the DVDs to Marjorie. At the same time, you can take the black umbrella to the Lost and Found since it's on the same floor. Also, there are some books in Arabic. They go to Level 2. Deliver the biography on Anwar Sadat to Level 3.

I was scheduled to give two presentations today. The first one is a workshop in Room C. Please put a sign on the door saying, "Today's workshop is canceled." I am also scheduled to read a book to the children. Please go to Children's Services and let Adishree know that I can't do it.

Because you are a new employee, I have attached a copy of the library directory to help you find your way around. Thank you again. I hope to recover quickly and see you at work tomorrow.

Hussein

Directory

Audiovisual (DVDs, Videos)	Level 1
Biography	Level 3
Children's Services	Level 5
Fiction	Level 3
Information Desk	Level 1
International Languages	Level 3
Lost and Found Items	Level 1
Music Research Collections	Level 6
Political Science	Level 2
Research Collection, A–M	Level 6
Research Collection, N–Z	Level 6
Security Desk	Level 1
Telephones	Level 1
Workshop Rooms	Level 4

181. Where does Marjorie work?

(A) Level 1
(B) Level 2
(C) Level 3
(D) Level 4

182. To which department should Olga take the Arabic books?

(A) Biography
(B) Fiction
(C) International Languages
(D) Political Science

183. Why should Olga put a sign on a door?

(A) To help children learn to read
(B) To tell library users that a workshop location has changed
(C) To inform people that Hussein can't give a presentation
(D) To let Adishree know that Hussein is out of the office today

184. Why does Olga need a library directory?

(A) She hasn't been working at the library for long.
(B) Several locations have changed recently.
(C) She has never been in the library before.
(D) People often get lost in the library.

185. What does Hussein plan to do tomorrow?

(A) Stay home
(B) Show Olga around the library
(C) Return to work
(D) Read a story to children

GO ON TO THE NEXT PAGE

Questions 186–190 refer to the following two e-mails.

From: Christina van Dijk
To: Heinz Niebaum
Subject: Meeting next week

Dear Heinz,
I am coming to Germany next Wednesday at 10:00 A.M. I will be at our office in Berlin. I am free on Thursday at 9:00 A.M. to go to Potsdam and meet with you. Are you available then?

I'd like to talk about ordering computer systems from your company. Our offices in Utrecht and Tillburg are expanding and need to upgrade their technology. I'd also like to meet with a trainer from your company so that we can work out a training package. Also, could you bring a training manual with you?

Let me know if you need me to bring anything. Also let me know if 9:00 isn't good for you. Maybe we can work something out later in the day.
Christina

From: Heinz Niebaum
To: Christina van Dijk
Subject: Re: Meeting next week

Christina,
I'm delighted that you're coming to Germany. It will be very convenient for us to meet because I will actually be in Potsdam from Tuesday through Friday, so we'll be able to meet at our office there on the day you suggested. The time you suggested is a bit early for me as I will be meeting with our CEO all morning. Are you available to meet at noon? Perhaps we could meet during lunch.

I will bring the materials that you requested. Theodor Eckert, our training supervisor, will join us. It would be helpful if you could bring some of your company's brochures and a copy of the annual report for us. Thank you.
Heinz

186. What does Christina want to discuss at the meeting with Heinz?

(A) Finding train schedules
(B) Buying computers
(C) Mailing packages
(D) Expanding office space

187. Where will Heinz and Christina meet?

(A) Berlin
(B) Potsdam
(C) Utrecht
(D) Tillburg

188. What day will they meet?

(A) Tuesday
(B) Wednesday
(C) Thursday
(D) Friday

189. Why can't Heinz see Christina at 9:00?

(A) He will be in another city.
(B) He has to pick up Mr. Eckert at the train station.
(C) He will be supervising a training session.
(D) He has to meet with someone else.

190. What will Heinz bring to the meeting with Christina?

(A) Some computers
(B) A training manual
(C) Some brochures
(D) An annual report

GO ON TO THE NEXT PAGE

Questions 191–195 refer to the following letter and purchase order.

Green Construction Co.
429 Mills Road
Minneapolis, MN 55440-0710
Tel: (763) 555-2100 Fax: (763) 555-2252

July 30, 20__

Sevil Tuncay
Construction Manager
National Bank
349 Taksim Square
Istanbul, Turkey 34400-4488

Dear Ms. Tuncay:

Thank you for contacting us to learn more about our environmentally friendly products. We suggest that you try a sample of our materials first. If you are happy with them, then you can buy more. If your order totals $10,000 or more, then we will reduce your shipping/handling fee by 3%. We prepared a purchase order for you so that you can try a sample of our products.

Our products may seem to cost more up front than other similar products. For example, you pay $200 more for our standard carpet than you would for a similar carpet that is not environmentally friendly. However, you save money in other ways. Because our carpets are made of special materials, they are much easier to clean and maintain.

One motion light is double the price of a regular light. However, motion lights save you money on electricity bills because the light stays on only when people are in the room. Also, the solar panels provide free energy. We suggest that you try the panels in several places on your building.

To buy the materials, please sign the purchase order. You may fax it to us, with your credit card number. We will ship the supplies immediately. Thank you for your business.

Yours truly,

Peter Lindstrom

Peter Lindstrom
Product Consultant

PURCHASE ORDER
Ship Prepaid—Add all delivery charges on invoice

National Bank
349 Taksim Square
Istanbul, Turkey 34400-4488

Tel: (212) 555-9890
Fax: (212) 555-9899

Vendor: Green Construction Co.
429 Mills Road
Minneapolis, MN 55440-0710
Tel: (763) 555-2100
Fax: (763) 555-2252

Ship To: Melike Paksoy
Purchasing Department
Address above

Reference: Purchase Order 22-385-06T
Date: 25 February 20__
Delivery Date: ASAP

Invoice To: Mert Miller
Accounting Department
Address above

Item	Model	Number	Quantity	Unit Cost	Total Cost
C84	Standard carpet	E569C	2	$500.00	$1000.00
M22	Motion lights	L230M	4	100.00	400.00
S76	Solar panels	L194S	4	200.00	800.00
Subtotal					2200.00
Shipping/Handling 10%					220.00
TOTAL					$2420.00

191. Who is the construction manager at the National Bank?

(A) Sevil Tuncay
(B) Peter Lindstrom
(C) Melike Paksoy
(D) Mert Miller

192. What is special about the products at Green Construction?

(A) They cost less than other companies' products.
(B) They don't harm the natural environment.
(C) They use more electricity than most other products.
(D) They can be ordered by fax.

193. How much does Green Construction charge for shipping on orders over $10,000?

(A) 3%
(B) 7%
(C) 10%
(D) 22%

194. What is the price of one standard carpet?

(A) $200
(B) $400
(C) $500
(D) $1000

195. What is the price of one regular light?

(A) $40
(B) $50
(C) $100
(D) $400

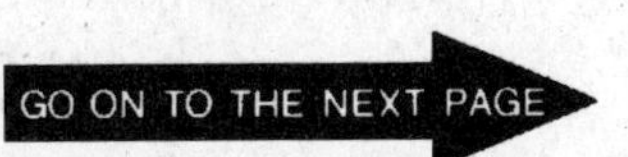

Questions 196–200 refer to the following agenda and fax.

Central Engineering Company
Board of Directors Meeting
Wednesday, November 15, 20__ 8:30 A.M.–11:30 A.M.
Place: Suite 10

AGENDA

1. Hiring challenges — Jorgen Spelman
2. Management changes — Narelle Dundee
3. Financial report — Madeira Jones
4. Technology upgrades — Jerry Carver

FAX COVER SHEET

CENTRAL ENGINEERING COMPANY
294 Green Street
Brasilia
Brazil

Tel: (55) 61 3420 4015
Fax: (55) 61 3420 4017

To: Ruben Baker
From: Narelle Dundee
Date: November 15, 20__
Pages: 1
Ref: Results of the board meeting
Message:

I hope your business trip is going well. Today's meeting went well for the most part, even though it began 30 minutes late. Jorgen wasn't there at the beginning, so I used his time slot to give my report. Jorgen finally arrived at 9:30 and gave his report. The board members were surprised to hear that job applicants complain about our salary offers. Jorgen's report really shocked and upset the board. Fortunately, Madeira's report had the opposite effect. Everyone was happy to hear about our great profits.

The technology upgrades report didn't go so well. Jerry had to leave the meeting before his report because there was an Internet problem in the Electrical Engineering department. Because of this, the presenter for our third agenda item read Jerry's report, and it was a bit confusing. She didn't really know what she was talking about and couldn't answer questions satisfactorily. We decided to ask Jerry to provide written answers to questions raised by board members during the meeting.

Because we started late, we finished a half hour late, but we still had to hurry to finish within the allotted time. We decided to make the next board meeting a half-hour longer to give more time for discussion and questions.

196. What time did the meeting start?

(A) 8:30
(B) 9:00
(C) 9:30
(D) 11:30

197. What was the topic of the first report given?

(A) Hiring challenges
(B) Management changes
(C) Finances
(D) Technology

198. How did people feel about the financial report?

(A) Dissatisfied
(B) Confused
(C) Happy
(D) Shocked

199. Who spoke about technology upgrades?

(A) Jerry Carver
(B) Narelle Dundee
(C) Madeira Jones
(D) Jorgen Spelman

200. What time was the meeting scheduled to end?

(A) 8:30
(B) 9:30
(C) 10:30
(D) 11:30

Stop! This is the end of the test. If you finish before time is called, you may go back to Parts 5, 6, and 7 and check your work.

PRACTICE TEST THREE

You will find the Answer Sheet for Practice Test Three on page 171. Detach it from the book and use it to record your answers. Play the audio for Practice Test Three when you are ready to begin.

LISTENING TEST

In the Listening test, you will be asked to demonstrate how well you understand spoken English. The entire Listening test will last approximately 45 minutes. There are four parts, and directions are given for each part. You must mark your answers on the separate answer sheet. Do not write your answers in the test book.

PART 1

Directions: For each question in this part, you will hear four statements about a picture in your test book. When you hear the statements, you must select the one statement that best describes what you see in the picture. Then find the number of the question on your answer sheet and mark your answer. The statements will not be printed in your test book and will be spoken only one time.

Sample Answer

Example

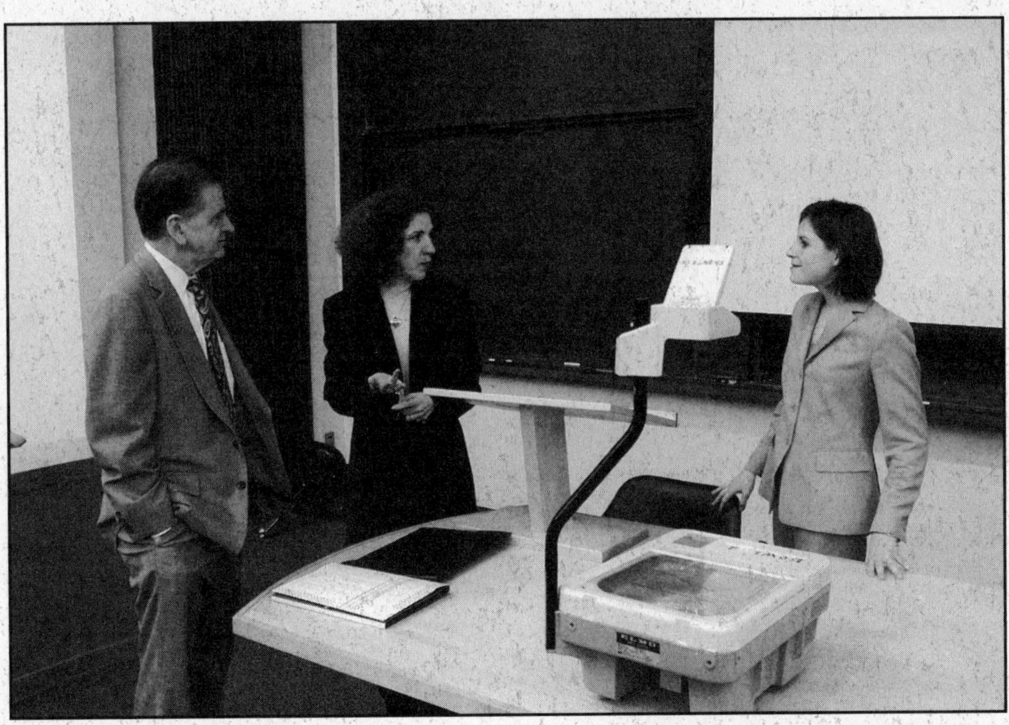

Statement (C), "They're standing near the table," is the best description of the picture, so you should select answer (C) and mark it on your answer sheet.

1. 

2. 

3.

4.

5. 

6. 

7.

8.

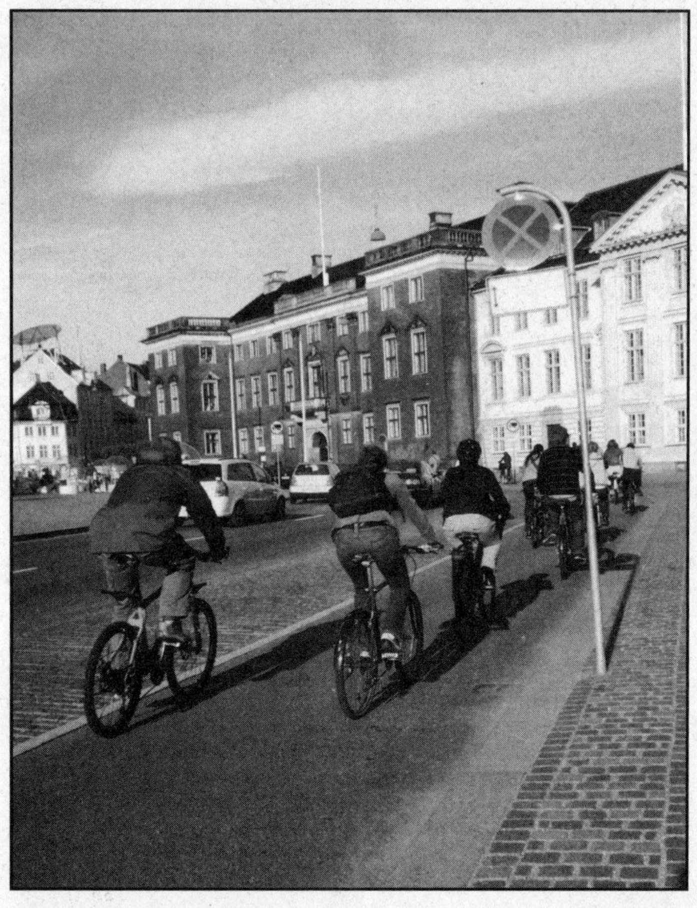

GO ON TO THE NEXT PAGE

9.

10.

PART 2

 **Directions:** You will hear a question or statement and three responses spoken in English. They will not be printed in your test book and will be spoken only one time. Select the best response to the question or statement and mark the letter (A), (B), or (C) on your answer sheet.

Sample Answer

 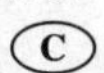

Example

You will hear: Where is the meeting room?

You will also hear:
(A) To meet the new director.
(B) It's the first room on the right.
(C) Yes, at two o'clock.

Your best response to the question "Where is the meeting room?" is choice (B), "It's the first room on the right," so (B) is the correct answer. You should mark answer (B) on your answer sheet.

11. Mark your answer on your answer sheet.

12. Mark your answer on your answer sheet.

13. Mark your answer on your answer sheet.

14. Mark your answer on your answer sheet.

15. Mark your answer on your answer sheet.

16. Mark your answer on your answer sheet.

17. Mark your answer on your answer sheet.

18. Mark your answer on your answer sheet.

19. Mark your answer on your answer sheet.

20. Mark your answer on your answer sheet.

21. Mark your answer on your answer sheet.

22. Mark your answer on your answer sheet.

23. Mark your answer on your answer sheet.

24. Mark your answer on your answer sheet.

25. Mark your answer on your answer sheet.

26. Mark your answer on your answer sheet.

27. Mark your answer on your answer sheet.

28. Mark your answer on your answer sheet.

29. Mark your answer on your answer sheet.

30. Mark your answer on your answer sheet.

31. Mark your answer on your answer sheet.

32. Mark your answer on your answer sheet.

33. Mark your answer on your answer sheet.

34. Mark your answer on your answer sheet.

35. Mark your answer on your answer sheet.

36. Mark your answer on your answer sheet.

37. Mark your answer on your answer sheet.

38. Mark your answer on your answer sheet.

39. Mark your answer on your answer sheet.

40. Mark your answer on your answer sheet.

GO ON TO THE NEXT PAGE

PART 3

Directions: You will hear some conversations between two people. You will be asked to answer three questions about what the speakers say in each conversation. Select the best response to each question and mark the letter (A), (B), (C), or (D) on your answer sheet. The conversations will not be printed in your test book and will be spoken only one time.

41. Where did the woman park the car?

(A) On the street.
(B) In the garage.
(C) In the parking lot.
(D) Next door.

42. How much does it cost to park?

(A) Two dollars an hour.
(B) Four dollars an hour.
(C) Five dollars an hour.
(D) Eight dollars an hour.

43. Where are the speakers going?

(A) To a class.
(B) To a movie.
(C) To a concert.
(D) To a soccer game.

---

44. Why didn't the man call the woman?

(A) He was away last week.
(B) He didn't feel well.
(C) He couldn't find the woman's number.
(D) He forgot.

45. What did the woman do last Saturday?

(A) She had a party.
(B) She went on a trip.
(C) She went to the doctor.
(D) She called the man.

46. What will the man do?

(A) Make a cake for the woman.
(B) Take the woman out for dinner.
(C) Buy the woman a birthday present.
(D) Give the woman some sweets.

---

47. What day does this conversation take place?

(A) Monday.
(B) Wednesday.
(C) Thursday.
(D) Saturday.

48. What did the man probably do last night?

(A) Watch TV.
(B) See some friends.
(C) Go out for dinner.
(D) Buy a watch.

49. What time does the woman usually get home?

(A) 1:00.
(B) 4:00.
(C) 6:00.
(D) 7:00.

---

50. What is the man's business?

(A) A farm.
(B) A restaurant.
(C) A flower shop.
(D) A grocery store.

51. How long has he had the business?

(A) Four years.
(B) Thirteen years.
(C) Fourteen years.
(D) Thirty years.

52. Where did he work before?

(A) At a hotel.
(B) At an office.
(C) At a hospital.
(D) At a car dealership.

---

53. Why are the speakers leaving?

(A) They are bored.
(B) The play is over.
(C) They fell asleep.
(D) They were told to leave.

54. How much did they pay for the tickets?

(A) $5.00.
(B) $17.50.
(C) $42.50
(D) $75.00.

55. What does the man want to do next time?

(A) Spend more money.
(B) Go to the movies.
(C) Invite a guest.
(D) Stay home.

---

56. Where are the speakers?

(A) At a tea party.
(B) At a night club.
(C) At a golf course.
(D) At a bowling alley.

57. What advice does the woman give the man?

(A) Swing hard.
(B) Stay calm.
(C) Join a club.
(D) Watch the ball.

58. What does the man want the woman to do?

(A) Hit the ball.
(B) Stop talking.
(C) Make a call.
(D) Stay out all night.

---

59. What time does the man's plane leave?

(A) Noon.
(B) 1:00.
(C) 3:00.
(D) 3:30.

60. How will he get to the airport?

(A) By subway.
(B) By car.
(C) By taxi.
(D) By bus.

61. When will he return?

(A) Sunday morning.
(B) Sunday night.
(C) Monday morning.
(D) Monday night.

---

62. Where does this conversation take place?

(A) By the door.
(B) In an elevator.
(C) In the woman's apartment.
(D) In the furniture department.

63. Which floor does the woman want to go to?

(A) Four.
(B) Seven.
(C) Eight.
(D) Eleven.

64. When will the sale end?

(A) Sunday.
(B) Monday.
(C) Tuesday.
(D) Friday.

65. Where does this conversation take place?

(A) At a pool.
(B) At a beach.
(C) At a school.
(D) At a racetrack.

66. What does the woman want to do?

(A) Put on a sweater.
(B) Sit in the sun.
(C) Have a race.
(D) Toss a ball.

67. How does the man feel?

(A) Old.
(B) Wet.
(C) Cold.
(D) Tired.

68. Where are the speakers going?

(A) To a park.
(B) To a hotel.
(C) To a bookstore.
(D) To a restaurant.

69. When do they have to be there?

(A) In fifteen minutes.
(B) In sixteen minutes.
(C) In fifty minutes.
(D) In sixty minutes.

70. What is the man afraid of?

(A) Getting lost.
(B) Being followed.
(C) Driving fast.
(D) Starting the car.

PART 4

Directions: You will hear some talks given by a single speaker. You will be asked to answer three questions about what the speaker says in each talk. Select the best response to each question and mark the letter (A), (B), (C), or (D) on your answer sheet. The talks will not be printed in your test book and will be spoken only one time.

71. What season is it?

(A) Spring.
(B) Summer.
(C) Fall.
(D) Winter.

72. What weather is expected this afternoon?

(A) Rain.
(B) Stormy winds.
(C) Cool breezes.
(D) Dry and windless.

73. When will the skies become clear again?

(A) Early in the afternoon.
(B) This evening.
(C) Tomorrow.
(D) Later in the week.

---

74. What day is Dr. Miller's office closed?

(A) Monday.
(B) Wednesday.
(C) Thursday.
(D) Friday.

75. Why would someone call 800-555-3212?

(A) To report an emergency.
(B) To pay a bill.
(C) To reschedule an exam.
(D) To get lab results.

76. How can someone speak with the doctor?

(A) Call back when the office is open.
(B) Call a different number.
(C) Leave a message.
(D) Visit the office on Monday.

---

77. What will the Stonebark Company do on March 1?

(A) Announce a new contest.
(B) Open its first branch in another country.
(C) Give customers a special discount.
(D) Expand its business into Asia.

78. What can Stonebark customers vote for?

(A) Their favorite flavor.
(B) Their favorite café.
(C) The location for a new café.
(D) Their favorite Stonebark employee.

79. What does the announcer say about the future of the Stonebark Company?

(A) It will not grow very fast.
(B) Its coffee will not be very special.
(C) Its future does not look very favorable.
(D) It will probably become popular around the world.

---

80. What does this store do?

(A) Rent computers only.
(B) Rent computers and office furniture.
(C) Rent and sell computers.
(D) Rent and repair computers only.

81. What is the minimum rental period?

(A) Hourly.
(B) Daily.
(C) Monthly.
(D) Yearly.

82. What time does the store close?

(A) 7:30.
(B) 8:30.
(C) 10:30.
(D) 11:30.

GO ON TO THE NEXT PAGE

83. What happened in Japan today?

(A) There was a riot.
(B) There was a tidal wave.
(C) There was a volcanic eruption.
(D) There was an earthquake.

84. When was the last time this happened in the same area?

(A) One month ago.
(B) Two months ago.
(C) Three months ago.
(D) One year ago.

85. How much damage was done to property?

(A) None.
(B) A little.
(C) Extensive.
(D) A great amount.

---

86. Where is the announcement being heard?

(A) At an airport.
(B) On a plane.
(C) At a consulate.
(D) At a bus station.

87. What is the gate number?

(A) 15.
(B) 16.
(C) 58.
(D) 60.

88. Who can go to the head of the line?

(A) People with passports.
(B) People with tickets.
(C) People with small bags.
(D) People with small children.

---

89. How many levels are reserved for employee parking?

(A) One.
(B) Two.
(C) Three.
(D) Four.

90. Which vehicles may park in the red spaces?

(A) Maintenance vehicles.
(B) Employees' cars.
(C) Visitors' cars.
(D) Two trucks.

91. What spaces are reserved for management?

(A) Yellow.
(B) Blue.
(C) White.
(D) Any space.

---

92. Who is listening to this announcement?

(A) Politicians.
(B) Guides.
(C) Diplomats.
(D) Tourists.

93. How is the group traveling?

(A) By van.
(B) By car.
(C) By bus.
(D) By train.

94. How long will the group stay at City Hall?

(A) Two hours.
(B) Three hours.
(C) Four hours.
(D) Five hours

---

95. What kind of sale is the bookstore having?

(A) Holiday.
(B) End-of-the-month.
(C) Back-to-school.
(D) Going-out-of-business.

96. What item is discounted 50 percent?

(A) Magazines.
(B) Calendars.
(C) CDs and DVDs.
(D) Paperback books.

97. What day is the bookstore closed?

(A) Saturday and Sunday.
(B) Sunday only.
(C) Sunday and Monday.
(D) Monday only.

98. What time will the sun set tonight?

(A) 5:00.
(B) 5:45.
(C) 8:00.
(D) 8:30.

99. What are small boats warned about?

(A) A foggy night.
(B) A windy evening.
(C) A rocky shore.
(D) An early sunset.

100. How will the weather be tomorrow afternoon?

(A) Windy.
(B) Snowy.
(C) Sunny.
(D) Rainy.

This is the end of the Listening test. Turn to Part 5 in your test book.

READING TEST

In the Reading test, you will read a variety of texts and answer several different types of reading comprehension questions. The entire Reading test will last 75 minutes. There are three parts, and directions are given for each part. You are encouraged to answer as many questions as possible within the time allowed.

You must mark your answers on the separate answer sheet. Do not write your answers in the test book.

PART 5

Directions: A word or phrase is missing in each of the sentences below. Four answer choices are given below each sentence. Select the best answer to complete the sentence. Then mark the letter (A), (B), (C), or (D) on your answer sheet.

101. A __________ firm will help us find software.

(A) consultation
(B) consultant
(C) consulting
(D) consult

102. __________ Mr. Jeffries to get the job done.

(A) Count on
(B) Count from
(C) Count in
(D) Count up

103. Ms. Nyguen had submitted her résumé before she __________ the position was filled.

(A) will know
(B) knows
(C) has known
(D) knew

104. If Mr. Donna were looking for a permanent job, our recruiter __________ help.

(A) may
(B) will
(C) can
(D) could

105. The purchaser wanted the equipment __________ by Monday morning.

(A) delivered
(B) delivering
(C) will be delivered
(D) must be delivered

106. The company's quarterly earnings were up; __________ the officers felt satisfied.

(A) nevertheless
(B) therefore
(C) however
(D) for this purpose

107. __________ substantial layoffs, costs were reduced.

(A) When
(B) Because of
(C) Although
(D) Since

108. Consumer confidence fell __________ April.

(A) next
(B) on
(C) in
(D) the

109. Price quotes __________.

(A) have daily been announced
(B) have been announced daily
(C) daily have been announced
(D) have been daily announced

110. The administration allows Thailand __________ Indonesia trade benefits.

(A) but
(B) nor
(C) and so
(D) and

111. The talks will take place __________ Brussels.

(A) at
(B) the
(C) in
(D) to

112. Many workers can't use computers; __________, training is required.

(A) on the whole
(B) besides
(C) consequently
(D) for example

113. If we had been __________ of the problem sooner, we might have been able to do something about it.

(A) aware
(B) awed
(C) awaken
(D) await

114. If our candidates __________ elected, we'll have a strong board.

(A) are
(B) were
(C) have been
(D) will be

115. It's important that the clients __________ interested.

(A) are seeming
(B) will seem
(C) is seeming
(D) seem

116. Find __________ the details and write a report.

(A) up
(B) about
(C) out
(D) around

117. The meeting __________ going on since eight o'clock this morning.

(A) has been
(B) was
(C) is
(D) will be

118. The consultant __________ his business if he had advertised.

(A) doubled
(B) will double
(C) would double
(D) could have doubled

119. Mr. Dalla would like the invoices __________ directly to Milan.

(A) fax
(B) faxing
(C) be faxed
(D) faxed

120. The members would resign if they __________ asked to do so.

(A) are
(B) were
(C) will be
(D) would be

121. Ambition, talent, __________ desire are ingredients for success.

(A) or
(B) never
(C) yet
(D) and

122. We need to be able to price our product so that it can __________ with other similar products in the marketplace.

(A) compete
(B) complete
(C) compute
(D) compote

123. The board reported that more funds __________ for training.

(A) was given
(B) could have given
(C) should be given
(D) is given

124. Some employees get their paychecks automatically __________ in their bank accounts.

(A) deposited
(B) depositing
(C) are deposited
(D) deposit

125. Costs should be cut; __________, the number of staff positions will be reduced.

(A) however
(B) therefore
(C) meanwhile
(D) but

126. Office branches are located __________ the metropolitan area.

(A) on
(B) at
(C) about
(D) throughout

127. The company offers a __________ plan for its workers.

(A) retirement
(B) retiring
(C) retire
(D) retired

128. __________ Mr. Hague finished the job interview, he felt relieved.

(A) While
(B) Because of
(C) During
(D) After

129. In order to apply for the position, you need to __________ a résumé and three letters of reference.

(A) compose
(B) reply
(C) submit
(D) peruse

130. The paychecks will be delivered __________ they arrive from the accounting department.

(A) before
(B) soon
(C) when
(D) during

131. The report outlines the products for the first quarter __________ the year.

(A) to
(B) at
(C) from
(D) of

132. The benefits package is impressive; __________, the director promotes only from within the company.

(A) for example
(B) when
(C) despite
(D) nevertheless

133. This company attempts to make its employees __________ like family.

(A) feeling
(B) feels
(C) felt
(D) feel

134. If Ms. Soto gets the salary __________ she has been hoping for, she will be able to buy a larger apartment.

(A) rise
(B) up
(C) raise
(D) more

135. The bank __________ another branch in Houston within the next year.

(A) opened
(B) will be opening
(C) have opened
(D) would open

136. Could you have the assistant __________ my office before he leaves today?

(A) stop off
(B) stop for
(C) stop to
(D) stop by

137. The office space we are interested in is large enough for our needs, but its __________ is terrible, so it will need a good deal of repair.

(A) condition
(B) location
(C) decoration
(D) imitation

138. Make sure to use an __________ dealer.

(A) authority
(B) authorization
(C) authorized
(D) authoritarian

139. The printer apologized for __________ two names on the program.

(A) leaving for
(B) leaving out
(C) leaving to
(D) leaving from

140. So many of the staff members __________ the plan that it was decided not to implement it.

(A) supposed
(B) opposed
(C) imposed
(D) reposed

GO ON TO THE NEXT PAGE

PART 6

Directions: Read the texts that follow. A word or phrase is missing in some of the sentences. Four answer choices are given below each of the sentences. Select the best answer to complete the text. Then mark the letter (A), (B), (C), or (D) on your answer sheet.

Questions 141–143 refer to the following memorandum.

From: Cheryl Milkov
To: Gary Bauers
Re: Vacation tasks

I have approved your request to take a vacation from December 20 to January 3. Please take care of the following before you leave.

1. For safety reasons, ________ all floor heaters and appliances, such as coffeemakers,

141. (A) unplug
(B) hook up
(C) activate
(D) refurbish

in your office. Turn off the lights and the computer. Close all windows.

2. Turn in your annual report to me. It should be ________ three and five pages in

142. (A) between
(B) until
(C) from
(D) for

length. Make sure to make a photocopy for yourself.

3. ________ your timesheet to the payroll office.

143. (A) Submission
(B) Submissive
(C) Submits
(D) Submit

4. Ask a co-worker to respond to your urgent phone calls. Leave a message on your voicemail system with your co-worker's phone number and your return date.

5. Add an "out-of-office message" to your e-mail system.

GO ON TO THE NEXT PAGE

Questions 144–146 refer to the following advertisement.

How would you like to save 50% on a rental car? Contact National Car Rental today!

You pay just half the usual rate on weekend rentals of compact cars. What a deal! But you have to hurry! This special ________ is available

144. (A) celebration
(B) expansion
(C) increase
(D) bargain

only for a short time.

National Car Rental also has luxury cars, trucks, and sports utility vehicles, and all are ________ with air-conditioning, a radio,

145. (A) equip
(B) equipped
(C) equipping
(D) equipment

and a CD player.

With offices at every major airport and in neighborhoods throughout the city, there is always a National Car Rental location close to you. Renting a car from us is easy.

Call now to reserve your ________ and be sure to ask about the

146. (A) suite
(B) vehicle
(C) voucher
(D) accommodation

50% discount. Note that this discount does not include insurance and is only available on certain weekends. Just go to our website to find the National Car Rental office closest to you!

Questions 147–149 refer to the following memorandum.

From: Jun Oh, Benefits Manager
To: Marcus Mains
Re: Special Retirement Opportunity

Thank you for requesting information about the Early Retirement Program. Please review these requirements. If you qualify, act quickly. Applications are due December 1.

Early Retirement Program

1. Employees must meet these _________ :

147. (A) requirements
(B) colleagues
(C) deadlines
(D) advisors

- Be age 50 with 20 years of employment at this company.
- OR have 25 years of employment at this company (age is not a factor). (Retirement funds are reduced by 2% for each year that you are under age 55.)

2. _________ employees should apply by December 1, 20__. The retirement

148. (A) Interest
(B) Interests
(C) Interested
(D) Interesting

program _________ on January 1, 20__.

149. (A) began
(B) will begin
(C) had begun
(D) have begun

3. Attend a workshop to learn more. E-mail my office to request the workshop schedule.

GO ON TO THE NEXT PAGE

Questions 150–152 refer to the following brochure.

Checklist for Starting Your Own Business

Are you thinking of starting your own business? Before you come up with a name and register your business, it's important to do a bit of homework. While most people think that starting a business is one of the most difficult things to do, this is actually not true. It is fairly easy to get a business started. The difficult part is keeping a business running, especially for the first few years. _________ off on the right foot is very

150. (A) Start
(B) Starting
(C) To start
(D) You start

important, however. This brochure will help you launch your business by following these steps.

Preparation: This section _________ you through the brainstorming

151. (A) guides
(B) controls
(C) promotes
(D) translates

process and helps you write a business plan. Learn to start thinking like an entrepreneur.

Hiring: Who can you trust to help you run a business? Here we will discuss the pros and cons of employing family and friends.

Maintaining Control: So you've got your business name and you've hired your staff. Now, you need to let everyone know who is boss and how _________ going to run.

152. (A) your operation
(B) is your operation
(C) your operation is
(D) will your operation

Expanding: You're following the plan and everything is going great. Are you ready to take your business to the next level? It's time to make a profit.

PART 7

Directions: In this part you will read a selection of texts, such as magazine and newspaper articles, letters, and advertisements. Each text is followed by several questions. Select the best answer for each question and mark the letter (A), (B), (C), or (D) on your answer sheet.

GO ON TO THE NEXT PAGE

Questions 153–155 refer to the following chart.

This chart shows how much the world's population grew between 1900 and 2000, and how much experts believe it will grow by 2025. The numbers are in billions.

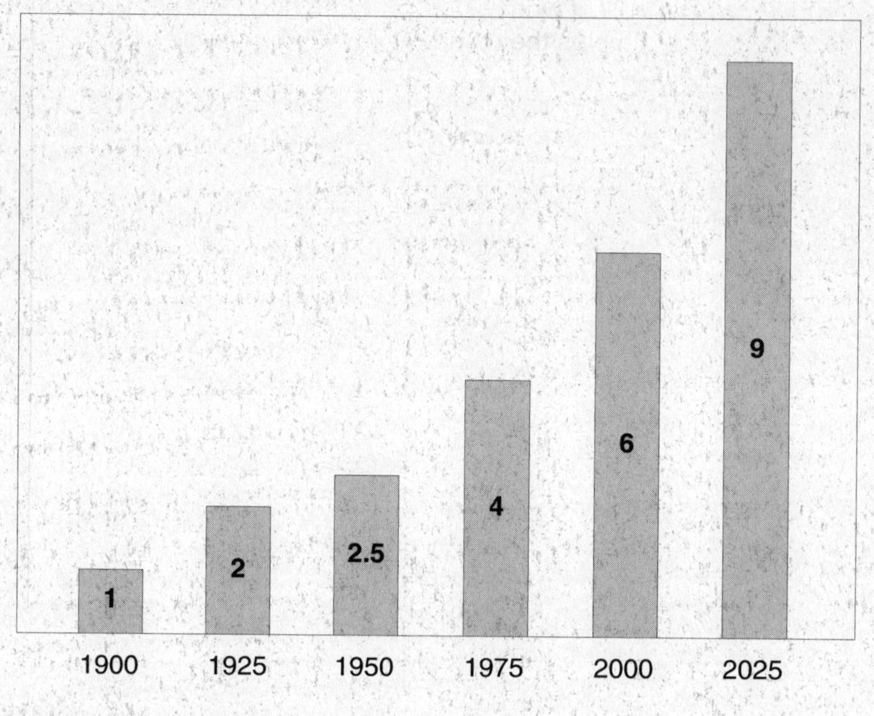

153. What was the world population in 1950?

(A) Half a billion
(B) 2 billion
(C) 2.5 billion
(D) 5 billion

154. In what year did the population reach 4 billion?

(A) 1900
(B) 1925
(C) 1950
(D) 1975

155. When was the population under 2 billion?

(A) In 1900
(B) In 1925
(C) In 1950
(D) In 1975

Questions 156–158 refer to the following article.

When a position becomes vacant, finding a new employee with the skill-set and personality that suit the needs of that particular workplace is a challenge that many companies face. First, the company must outline the tasks and responsibilities involved in the position to be filled. A careful analysis of these will help the company define what skills, abilities, and knowledge an employee must have in order to carry out the job successfully. Often it is the process of writing the job description and vacancy announcement that helps the company define the qualities they seek in a new employee.

Once the requirements of the position are defined, the next challenge is to find the person who can meet those requirements. One of the most common ways to locate a qualified person to fill a vacant position is to look within the organization itself. Is anyone currently working for the company who could do the job? This is often the best way to find qualified people. They are already known to the company, have been successful in it, and are familiar with its people, procedures, and policies.

If there is no available person within the company who is qualified to fill the vacancy, then someone must be sought outside the organization. Some of the most common sources of new employees are educational institutions such as high schools, junior colleges, four-year colleges, and universities. Companies also use newspapers and industry association newsletters to help locate job applicants.

156. What is this article about?

(A) Reading newspapers
(B) Hiring employees
(C) Protecting the organization
(D) Going to high school

157. What is an example of a common outside source?

(A) High schools
(B) Resources within the organization
(C) Spies
(D) Temporary employees

158. According to the passage, what do firms use to help locate applicants?

(A) Yellow pages
(B) Subway ads
(C) Newspaper ads
(D) Word of mouth

GO ON TO THE NEXT PAGE

Questions 159–161 refer to the following announcement.

AERONAUTIC SYSTEMS, INC., the Berlin-based company also known as AeroSys, has made an agreement with three of the world's major international airlines to provide a satellite system for voice and data communications, a company spokesperson announced last week. This agreement is a major leap forward for the company, which began operations just three years ago and has now gained the business of three of the airline industry's largest companies.

The agreement with Skyways, Air One, and Travelers International will provide communications between aircraft and on-ground systems for operational control and air-traffic services. The agreement was signed last month, and AeroSys will begin providing services to the airlines before the end of the year.

159. Where is AeroSys based?

(A) In London
(B) In New York
(C) In Berlin
(D) In Tokyo

160. According to the passage, what will be provided by the agreement?

(A) Aircraft
(B) A satellite system
(C) On-ground systems
(D) Air traffic services

161. Which of the following is NOT a part of this agreement?

(A) A satellite system
(B) Communication between aircraft
(C) A system of voice and data communication
(D) Ticketing service

Questions 162–165 refer to the following announcement.

San Juan Academy has developed a unique approach to dealing with underachieving students. Instead of doling out punishment for incomplete assignments, or assigning extra hours of tutoring for bad grades, the academy provides failing students with a reward. Through the Computers for Success program, San Juan Academy students who fall behind their classmates in reading and mathematics are given their own computers. For nine weeks, the students get to keep a personal computer with a printer and software in their homes. They can work and play with the computer whenever they like and as often as they like.

Is this a prize for being bad in school? "It may look that way to an outsider," says school principal Edna Seymour, "but this approach is actually well-backed up by research. Studies show that students who are computer literate do much better in school. The figures rise for students who actually have a computer at home, and are even higher for students from homes where most of the family members are comfortable using a computer."

Because of this, when a student is given a computer to take home, families are encouraged to get into the act, too. Students in the Computers for Success program are required, together with their parents and siblings, to attend a weekend computer seminar. This way everyone in the family becomes familiar with the use of the computer. This is an investment in the students' educational future. "It is widely accepted that parental involvement makes all the difference in a child's school success," says Principal Seymour. "We are extending that idea to involve families in our computer literacy program. As part of that program, we make it possible for families to buy refurbished computers at an affordable price. Many of our families have already taken advantage of this opportunity. On the whole, we have been very pleased with the Computers for Success program."

162. Which of the following is NOT part of the program?

(A) Software programs
(B) A printer
(C) A personal computer
(D) Textbooks

163. When can students use the computers?

(A) Only during school time
(B) On weekends only
(C) At lunch break
(D) Anytime they wish

164. What are families of the students encouraged to do?

(A) Become involved
(B) Be actors
(C) Drive away
(D) Donate computers

165. The word "siblings" in paragraph 3, line 3, is closest in meaning to

(A) classmates
(B) brothers and sisters
(C) teachers
(D) friends and neighbors

Questions 166–169 refer to the following article.

We most often think of communication as talking, but it commonly occurs in other forms as well. In addition to words, communication can occur in the form of pictures or through actions.

When we speak or write, we are using words to communicate our ideas and feelings. It is essential for people to use words effectively in order to communicate clearly. Although words may seem straightforward, they are as subject to misinterpretation as any other form of communication.

Pictures can be a quite powerful form of communication. You will understand this if you think of any great work of art. Businesses can successfully use pictures in posters, charts, signs, and packaging. When combining words and pictures, the design should be carefully planned out. The pictures used on posters and charts, as well as in brochures and advertisements, should complement rather than conflict with the words.

Action is an important form of communication that we are often unaware of. As the adage says, "Actions speak louder than words." This medium is most important when dealing face-to-face with employees, colleagues, and clients. A frown, a handshake, a wink, and even silence all have meaning and people will attach significance to these actions. Just as it is important to choose our words carefully, it is also important to be aware of our actions and of how they may be perceived by others.

166. What is the main topic of the article?

(A) Marketing
(B) Communication
(C) Actions
(D) Businesses

167. According to the article, which of the following is used the most?

(A) Words
(B) Posters
(C) Charts
(D) Telephones

168. The word "medium" in paragraph 4, line 3, is closest in meaning to

(A) size
(B) method
(C) situation
(D) movement

169. Which of the following is NOT given as an example of actions?

(A) Silence
(B) A wink
(C) Television
(D) A handshake

Questions 170–171 refer to the following announcement.

Responding to the needs of an aging population, Health Network, Inc. of Melbourne and Futura Computing of Perth Amboy have agreed to cooperate in the development of handheld, computerized products to help the elderly monitor their health. It is widely accepted in the health-care field that patients who participate in monitoring their health status enjoy healthier lives. They are more aware of the factors affecting their health and are better-informed participants in making decisions regarding their health care. It is expected that these products will go a long way toward improving the health of senior citizens.

The cost of these products to the individual consumer will be covered under most insurance plans. They will be made available free or at reduced cost to low-income senior citizens who qualify according to government guidelines.

170. Who would most likely read this announcement?

(A) Lawyers
(B) Health-care professionals
(C) Word processors
(D) Teachers

171. Which of the following could be one of the products?

(A) Dishwashers
(B) Calculators
(C) Blood-pressure monitors
(D) All-weather gloves

Questions 172–173 refer to the following announcement.

Operation of Detroit's trash incinerator, the largest in the nation, was halted last month, less than a year after it was put into service. The huge plant, which was designed to change waste into energy, had been hailed as an innovative means of putting trash to good use. However, soon after the plan began operating, unhealthy levels of mercury began to be detected in the air around the city. It was soon discovered that the culprit was the new incinerator. Entire neighborhoods were threatened by the toxins being discharged into the air. Environmental officials ordered the plant to be shut down last week. They say it is uncertain when, or even whether, the plant will reopen.

172. According to the passage, why was the plant shut down?

(A) There was too much trash.
(B) It was unhealthy.
(C) It was unable to convert waste into energy.
(D) It could not be regulated.

173. What was the function of the plant?

(A) To collect waste
(B) To monitor air quality
(C) To supply Detroit with mercury
(D) To turn trash into energy

GO ON TO THE NEXT PAGE

Questions 174–177 refer to the following article.

Absenteeism is an ongoing problem in many companies, and the Stummering Corporation was no exception. Absenteeism and late arrival had been issues there for a long time, so management decided to study the problem. During the months of January through June of this year, employee absentee rates and arrival times were monitored. It was discovered that the average employee was showing up for work fifteen minutes late three times a week. In addition, the study showed that the majority of employees were missing a minimum of one day of work per month. Aside from the direct effects this situation was having on productivity, it was also creating a noticeable impact on employee morale. Management knew that this was a serious problem and that something had to be done right away.

Human Resources suggested that management undertake an incentive program. A plan was devised whereby every employee who arrived at work on time every day during the month of August would be eligible for a cash award. Within five days of the announcement, the number of late arrivals had declined to the lowest level the company had ever experienced. The company decided to extend the program so that employees who didn't miss any days of work for the rest of the year (exclusive of approved vacations) would also be eligible for a cash award. As a result, absenteeism declined dramatically. Stummering plans to continue the program into next year and is looking into making it permanent company policy. This successful program could easily be replicated at other companies. It worked for Stummering. It could work for you.

174. What was the problem at the Stummering Corporation?

(A) Management
(B) Absenteeism
(C) Low pay
(D) Unprofessional atmosphere

175. How many times was the average employee late?

(A) Three times a week
(B) Fifteen times a week
(C) Three times between January and June
(D) Fifteen times between January and June

176. What did employees who were on time receive?

(A) A vacation
(B) A cash award
(C) A promotion
(D) A new watch

177. The word "replicated" in paragraph 2, line 10, is closest in meaning to

(A) copied
(B) enjoyed
(C) studied
(D) announced

Questions 178–180 refer to the following letter.

WALTERS CORPORATION
3255 Trenton Avenue, Columbus, OH 43216

November 20, 20__

Mr. Alan Porter
2870 Kennewick Drive
Bloomington, IN 42777

Dear Mr. Porter,

We were pleased to receive your letter and résumé inquiring about the vacant position which we announced in the *Journal of Engineering and Business* last month. Unfortunately, your letter arrived on my desk several days after the closing date of November 1. We received an overwhelming response to our job announcement. There were over 25 applications from qualified accountants. Although you appear to be well qualified for the position we announced, I am sorry to inform you that we have already hired another applicant. However, we were impressed with your background, and we would like to keep your résumé on file. We anticipate hiring again in the spring or summer of next year. We will inform you when another position that matches your qualifications becomes vacant.

We wish you the best of luck in your job search.

Thank you for your interest in the Walters Corporation.

Sincerely,

John Simons

John Simons
Director of Human Resources

178. What is the main purpose of the letter?

(A) To ask for a job
(B) To reject someone who wanted a job
(C) To ask for references
(D) To learn about the Walters Corporation

179. What did Mr. Porter include with his letter?

(A) His résumé
(B) A report on the Walters Corporation
(C) A gift for Mr. Simons
(D) A job announcement

180. What is Mr. Porter's profession?

(A) Director of Human Resources
(B) Detective
(C) Accountant
(D) Administrative Assistant

Questions 181–185 refer to the following forms.

DATE: June 19, 20__ TIME: 5:15 A.M. (P.M.)

FOR:

RECEIVED BY: Lev

CALLER: Marina

PHONE NUMBER: (3272) 43-98-58

MESSAGE: She immediately needs 2 computers, 10 packs of ink cartridges, 5 standard phones, and 2 photocopiers: 1 industrial-sized and 1 personal-sized. She also needs furniture: 2 large wooden desks, 4 small wooden chairs, 1 tall metal filing cabinet, and 1 long metal meeting table. She can wait 7 days for the furniture. Please call her back to confirm fulfillment of this order.

CALL BACK REQUESTED? (YES) NO

DATE/TIME COMPLETED: ___/___/___ ___:___ A.M. P.M.

DATE: June 20, 20__ TIME: 9:20 (A.M.) P.M.

FOR: Marina

RECEIVED BY: Konstantin

CALLER: Alonya

PHONE NUMBER: (095) 555-45-03

MESSAGE: Most of those items are here in Moscow. There will be a three-day delay on the large copier. Also, she will have to order the table from Almaty, so it will arrive 1 day after your deadline. Let her know if that's OK. Express shipping is possible. She can explain the charges for that if you are interested. Call her back today to order. She's headed to Berlin tomorrow, then on to Paris later in the week, so this has to be taken care of today.

CALL BACK REQUESTED? (YES) NO

DATE/TIME COMPLETED: ___/___/___ ___:___ A.M. P.M.

181. Who is ordering office supplies?

(A) Lev
(B) Marina
(C) Konstantin
(D) Alonya

182. What kind of filing cabinet does the caller want?

(A) Standard
(B) Personal-sized
(C) Wooden
(D) Metal

183. Where are the ink cartridges now?

(A) Moscow
(B) Almaty
(C) Berlin
(D) Paris

184. When will the table arrive?

(A) One day after it was ordered
(B) Two days after it was ordered
(C) Seven days after it was ordered
(D) Eight days after it was ordered

185. What will Alonya do tomorrow?

(A) Call Marina
(B) Ship the order
(C) Leave on a trip
(D) Buy a table

GO ON TO THE NEXT PAGE

Questions 186–190 refer to the following e-mail and table.

From: Guillermo Grimaldi
To: Samantha Young
Subject: Survey Results

We have the results of our Preferred Investments Survey. I have attached the "Types of Investments" table.

There is one change on the survey compared to last year. We divided one major category into two parts. The parts are "buildings" and "property." That's why we don't have a number from last year to use as a comparison.

We talked to 1,000 investors between March 1 and March 15. While most of them put their money into a variety of investments, the survey shows that this year there was a greater variety in the type of investment chosen than last year. More people are purchasing each different type of investment. For example, look at the number of mutual fund investors last year (800) as compared to this year (850).

These results will help our company better decide how to sell our investment products. We predict three types of investment will increase in popularity, and they should be heavily advertised over the next year. Also, we predict that three investments will decrease in popularity. We should decide what to do about those. Are you available on Friday morning? Let's discuss the declining investments.

Types of Investments
March 1–15

	Number of Investors (this year)	Number of Investors (last year)	Prediction*
Annuity	825	815	s
Bonds	1,000	850	s
Cash	1,000	1,000	s
Gold	625	600	d
IRA 900	875	—	d
IRA, Roth	975	900	u
Mutual Fund	850	800	s
Real Estate, buildings	987	—	d
Real Estate, property	700	—	u
Savings	1,000	1,000	s
Stocks, domestic	945	936	s
Stocks, international	965	900	u

*Prediction: d=will go down; s=will stay the same; u=will go up

186. How many investors participated in the survey?

(A) 800
(B) 850
(C) 965
(D) 1,000

187. How many survey participants invested in gold this year?

(A) 600
(B) 625
(C) 900
(D) 875

188. Why are three categories on the table missing numbers from last year?

(A) Nobody invested in those areas last year.
(B) People lost all their money in those investments.
(C) Real estate was not divided into two categories last year.
(D) The survey did not ask about real estate investments.

189. Which types of investment does Mr. Grimaldi want to advertise?

(A) Bonds, cash, and savings
(B) Gold, Roth IRAs, and mutual funds
(C) Annuities, domestic stocks, and real estate
(D) Roth IRAs, real estate, and international stocks

190. Which types of investments does Mr. Grimaldi want to discuss with Ms. Young?

(A) Gold, IRA 900's, and real estate
(B) International and domestic stocks
(C) Cash, savings, and bonds
(D) Mutual funds, Roth IRAs, and annuities

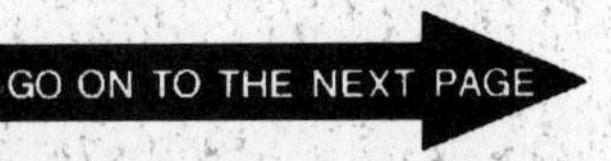

Questions 191–195 refer to the following advertisement and e-mail.

THE 20TH ANNUAL HOME ELECTRONICS SHOW

January 20–24

Join us at the Convention Center to see the latest in home electronics. Companies from around the country will display new model stereos, TVs, and sound systems for home use, as well as the latest in home security devices. Don't miss the special domestic robot demonstrations. See robots clean floors, wash dishes, even take out the garbage!

Admission to the show costs $10 for adults, $5 for children ages 5–12. Children under 5 will not be admitted. An extra $3 fee is charged for some special events. These include:

January 21	Movie: "The Home of Tomorrow"
January 22	Speaker: Roberta Wilkinson, President of Automation, Inc. Topic: The invention team at Automation, Inc.
January 23	Demonstration: Home Security Systems
January 24	Reception with JET Company, the Designers of RoboCleaners

Tickets can be purchased at the Convention Center or online. There is an extra charge of $1 per ticket for online purchases.
Buy your tickets today! Last year's show sold out!

From: Mai Itakura
To: Hank Ellmers
Sent: Wednesday, January 19, 20__ 11:12 P.M.
Subject: Schedule a time to go to the show

Hank,
The Home Electronics Show begins tomorrow and lasts through the weekend. Would you like to go with me? Your daughter Emma might enjoy it, too. It would cost just $25 for the three of us.

We can go tomorrow or later in the week if you prefer. There are some special events that you might enjoy, too. That company that you just bought stock in is giving a presentation on January 22. The company's president is speaking. You will probably want to see the security demonstration, too, since you're a police officer.

E-mail or call me today if you're interested. I'll be near the Convention Center tomorrow, so I can pick up the tickets without paying the extra charge. By the way, there is also an extra charge for the special events. You pay it at the time of each event, so you can decide about that later.
Mai

191. What will robots demonstrate at the convention?

(A) Playing stereos
(B) Watching TV
(C) Doing housework
(D) Operating security systems

192. When can convention visitors see a movie?

(A) January 20
(B) January 21
(C) January 22
(D) January 23

193. How old is Emma?

(A) Younger than five
(B) Between five and twelve
(C) Older than twelve
(D) Eighteen

194. In what company does Hank own stock?

(A) Automation, Inc.
(B) Home Security Systems
(C) JET Company
(D) RoboCleaners

195. How much extra will Hank pay to see the security demonstration?

(A) $1.00
(B) $3.00
(C) $5.00
(D) $10.00

GO ON TO THE NEXT PAGE

Questions 196–200 refer to the following e-mail messages.

To: Gertrude Gerlak
From: Ping Lai
Subject: Retirement party

Hi Gertrude,
Don't forget that Samir's party is tomorrow night at the Lotus Chinese restaurant at 7:00. I'm giving Rae a ride. Let me know today if you want to ride with us. We plan to leave here at 6:15 so we can get to the restaurant on time to put up some decorations before everyone else arrives. I hope you don't mind helping with that. In fact, we would really appreciate your help since you have such an artistic eye. Rae has a card for Samir already, and she is collecting money for a gift. Let her know if you have any ideas for the gift. Thanks.
Ping

To: Ping Lai
From: Gertrude Gerlak
Subject: Re: Retirement party

Hi Ping,
Yes, I need a ride. Thanks for the offer. I went to the Lotus restaurant last month for my birthday. It's a great place. I don't mind leaving here early, and I'm happy to help with the decorations. Alex needs a ride, too, if you have enough room in your car for all of us. Do you need me to buy any decorations? Why don't we leave thirty minutes earlier than you said? That way we're sure to have enough time to do some really nice decorating. I'll be in a meeting tomorrow afternoon, but it should be over well before we have to leave. I think a digital camera would be a great gift. Tell Rae I'll pick one up tomorrow during my lunch hour. I know where I can get a great price on one. She can give me the money later.
Gertrude

196. Why are Ping and Gertrude going to a restaurant tomorrow?

(A) For a birthday party
(B) For a work meeting
(C) For a retirement party
(D) For a monthly get-together

197. How many people want to ride with Ping?

(A) One
(B) Two
(C) Three
(D) Four

198. What time does Gertrude want to leave for the party?

(A) 5:45
(B) 6:15
(C) 6:30
(D) 7:00

199. Who will receive a digital camera?

(A) Rae
(B) Ping
(C) Alex
(D) Samir

200. Why will Rae give money to Gertrude?

(A) To pay for dinner
(B) To pay for the gift
(C) To pay for decorations
(D) To pay for a ride

Stop! This is the end of the test. If you finish before time is called, you may go back to Parts 5, 6, and 7 and check your work.

PRACTICE TEST FOUR

You will find the Answer Sheet for Practice Test Four on page 173. Detach it from the book and use it to record your answers. Play the audio for Practice Test Four when you are ready to begin.

LISTENING TEST

In the Listening test, you will be asked to demonstrate how well you understand spoken English. The entire Listening test will last approximately 45 minutes. There are four parts, and directions are given for each part. You must mark your answers on the separate answer sheet. Do not write your answers in the test book.

PART 1

Directions: For each question in this part, you will hear four statements about a picture in your test book. When you hear the statements, you must select the one statement that best describes what you see in the picture. Then find the number of the question on your answer sheet and mark your answer. The statements will not be printed in your test book and will be spoken only one time.

Sample Answer

Example

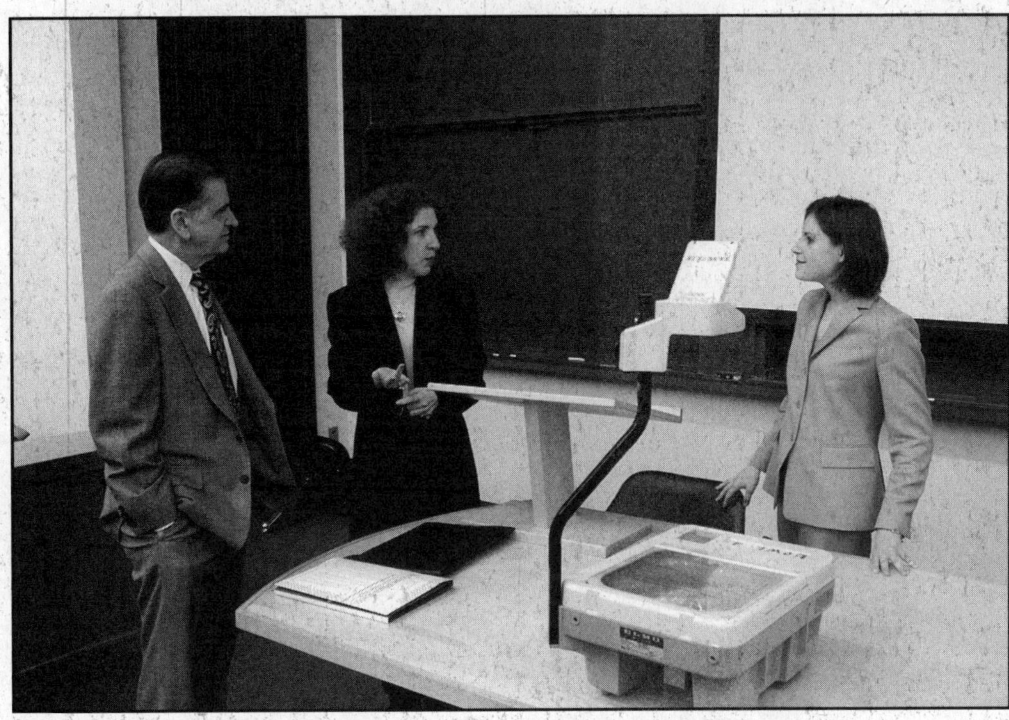

Statement (C), "They're standing near the table," is the best description of the picture, so you should select answer (C) and mark it on your answer sheet.

1.

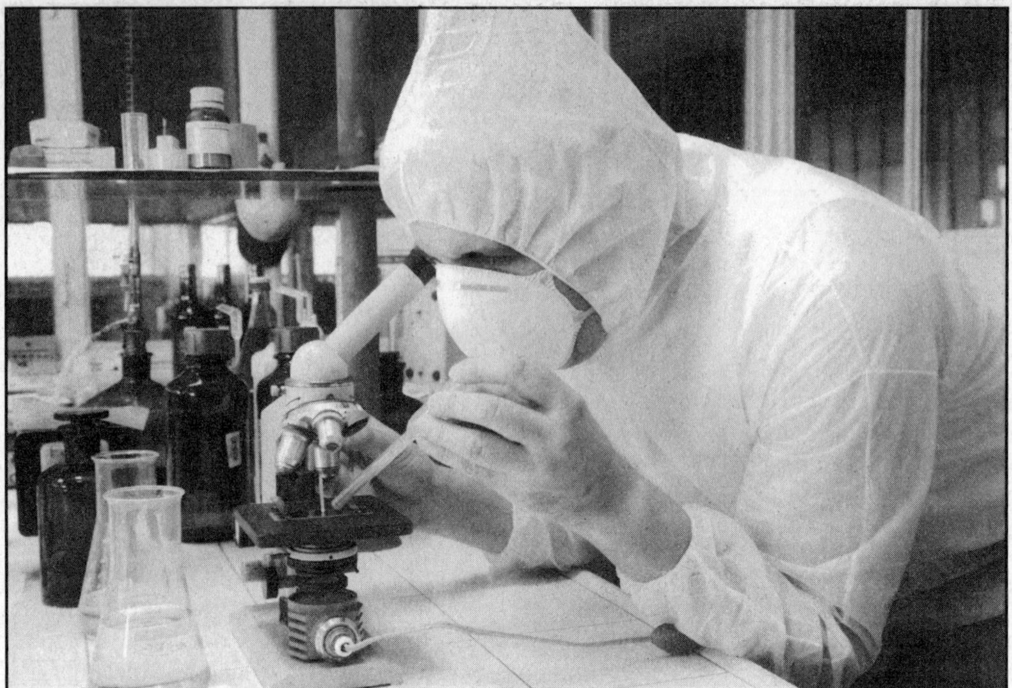

2.

3.

4.

GO ON TO THE NEXT PAGE

5.

6.

7.

8.

GO ON TO THE NEXT PAGE

9.

10.

PART 2

Directions: You will hear a question or statement and three responses spoken in English. They will not be printed in your test book and will be spoken only one time. Select the best response to the question or statement and mark the letter (A), (B), or (C) on your answer sheet.

Sample Answer

Example

You will hear: Where is the meeting room?

You will also hear:
(A) To meet the new director.
(B) It's the first room on the right.
(C) Yes, at two o'clock.

Your best response to the question "Where is the meeting room?" is choice (B), "It's the first room on the right," so (B) is the correct answer. You should mark answer (B) on your answer sheet.

11. Mark your answer on your answer sheet.

12. Mark your answer on your answer sheet.

13. Mark your answer on your answer sheet.

14. Mark your answer on your answer sheet.

15. Mark your answer on your answer sheet.

16. Mark your answer on your answer sheet.

17. Mark your answer on your answer sheet.

18. Mark your answer on your answer sheet.

19. Mark your answer on your answer sheet.

20. Mark your answer on your answer sheet.

21. Mark your answer on your answer sheet.

22. Mark your answer on your answer sheet.

23. Mark your answer on your answer sheet.

24. Mark your answer on your answer sheet.

25. Mark your answer on your answer sheet.

26. Mark your answer on your answer sheet.

27. Mark your answer on your answer sheet.

28. Mark your answer on your answer sheet.

29. Mark your answer on your answer sheet.

30. Mark your answer on your answer sheet.

31. Mark your answer on your answer sheet.

32. Mark your answer on your answer sheet.

33. Mark your answer on your answer sheet.

34. Mark your answer on your answer sheet.

35. Mark your answer on your answer sheet.

36. Mark your answer on your answer sheet.

37. Mark your answer on your answer sheet.

38. Mark your answer on your answer sheet.

39. Mark your answer on your answer sheet.

40. Mark your answer on your answer sheet.

GO ON TO THE NEXT PAGE

PART 3

Directions: You will hear some conversations between two people. You will be asked to answer three questions about what the speakers say in each conversation. Select the best response to each question and mark the letter (A), (B), (C), or (D) on your answer sheet. The conversations will not be printed in your test book and will be spoken only one time.

41. What is the man looking for?

(A) Papers.
(B) Cups.
(C) Ink bottles.
(D) Pen caps.

42. Where are the things that he is looking for?

(A) In the cabinet.
(B) Under the sink.
(C) Over the sink.
(D) In the closet.

43. What does the man want to do?

(A) Drink some tea.
(B) Write a letter.
(C) Go to the coffee shop.
(D) Buy some sugar.

---

44. Where does this conversation take place?

(A) At home
(B) At a bank.
(C) At a hotel.
(D) At an airport.

45. What time does the man have to leave?

(A) 2:00.
(B) 5:00.
(C) 5:30.
(D) 10:00.

46. When will the man pay his bill?

(A) Now.
(B) At noon.
(C) Tonight.
(D) In the morning.

---

47. How does the man get to work?

(A) He walks.
(B) He takes a bus.
(C) He rides a train.
(D) He drives a car.

48. How many times has he been late this month?

(A) Two.
(B) Three.
(C) Four.
(D) Eight.

49. What will he do tomorrow?

(A) Stay until 9:00.
(B) Get to work on time.
(C) Talk to the boss.
(D) Take a rest.

---

50. What does the woman want to borrow?

(A) Money for lunch.
(B) A screwdriver.
(C) A paperback book.
(D) A toolbox.

51. When will she return it?

(A) Before lunch.
(B) After lunch.
(C) In the afternoon.
(D) Tonight.

52. Where will she put it?

(A) In the closet.
(B) On the chair.
(C) On the man's desk.
(D) In the man's backpack.

---

53. How long is the man's vacation?

(A) One week.
(B) Two weeks.
(C) Three weeks.
(D) Four weeks.

54. When will he take his vacation?

(A) August.
(B) September.
(C) November.
(D) December.

55. What will he do on his vacation?

(A) Clean the house.
(B) Swim.
(C) Visit different cities.
(D) Sit on the beach.

---

56. What is the woman buying?

(A) Shoes.
(B) Shirts.
(C) Skirts.
(D) Hats.

57. Which color does she choose?

(A) Green.
(B) White.
(C) Blue.
(D) Gray.

58. How much does she have to pay?

(A) $16.
(B) $32.
(C) $25.
(D) $50.

---

59. In which direction does the man want to go?

(A) Left.
(B) Right.
(C) Forward.
(D) Backward.

60. What time is it now?

(A) 6:10.
(B) 6:15.
(C) 6:45.
(D) 7:00.

61. Where are the speakers going?

(A) To a ball game.
(B) To lunch.
(C) To a concert.
(D) To the park.

---

62. Where are the brochures?

(A) In Singapore.
(B) In the supply room.
(C) In the mail.
(D) At the printer.

63. When does the woman need the brochures?

(A) This morning.
(B) This afternoon.
(C) Tonight.
(D) Tomorrow morning.

64. How many brochures does the woman need?

(A) Twenty.
(B) One hundred.
(C) Two hundred.
(D) One thousand.

GO ON TO THE NEXT PAGE

65. What time was the meeting today?

(A) 2:00.
(B) 3:00.
(C) 6:00.
(D) 9:00.

66. Why wasn't the woman at the meeting?

(A) She had to make a call.
(B) She forgot about it.
(C) She was busy.
(D) She was sick.

67. When is the next meeting?

(A) Tuesday.
(B) Wednesday.
(C) Thursday.
(D) Friday.

68. What is the man doing now?

(A) Going to work.
(B) Driving his car.
(C) Eating breakfast.
(D) Reading a letter.

69. How is the weather now?

(A) Sunny.
(B) Rainy.
(C) Cool.
(D) Icy.

70. How will the woman get to school?

(A) By car.
(B) By bus.
(C) On foot.
(D) By train.

PART 4

Directions: You will hear some talks given by a single speaker. You will be asked to answer three questions about what the speaker says in each talk. Select the best response to each question and mark the letter (A), (B), (C), or (D) on your answer sheet. The talks will not be printed in your test book and will be spoken only one time.

71. Why is the airport closed?

(A) Because of heavy traffic.
(B) Because of heavy fog.
(C) Because of strong winds.
(D) Because of falling snow.

72. When will the airport reopen?

(A) By this morning.
(B) By noon.
(C) By early evening.
(D) By late evening.

73. What should passengers on today's flights do?

(A) Go to the airport.
(B) Leave the airport.
(C) Call their airline.
(D) Call the Weather Center.

---

74. What time does the train arrive in New York?

(A) 9:30.
(B) 2:40.
(C) 6:00.
(D) 6:15.

75. How many stops does the train make?

(A) None.
(B) One.
(C) Two.
(D) Six.

76. Who is not allowed on the train?

(A) Passengers who are late.
(B) Passengers with excess luggage.
(C) Passengers without reservations.
(D) Passengers who don't pay by check.

---

77. What is offered to guests who make their reservations on the hotel's website?

(A) A book.
(B) A discount.
(C) A meal.
(D) A photo.

78. Which of the following can be found on the hotel's website?

(A) Guest room prices.
(B) The restaurant menu.
(C) The conference schedule.
(D) Club membership information.

79. What service does the hotel offer?

(A) Catering.
(B) Exercise training.
(C) Conference planning.
(D) Website design.

---

80. Where is this announcement being heard?

(A) In a restaurant.
(B) In a school room.
(C) In a meeting room.
(D) At a train station.

81. What time will the session resume?

(A) 10:15.
(B) 10:30.
(C) 10:45.
(D) 11:00.

82. What did the participants just finish?

(A) The question-and-answer period.
(B) A coffee break.
(C) Their résumé.
(D) Ms. Johnson's report.

GO ON TO THE NEXT PAGE

83. What is the problem?

(A) High waters.
(B) Lack of food.
(C) More homes than families.
(D) Expensive property.

84. How many people have died?

(A) None.
(B) Twenty.
(C) Thousands.
(D) Millions.

85. When will the president visit the area?

(A) On Sunday.
(B) On Monday.
(C) On Friday.
(D) On Saturday.

---

86. What does Carlos do?

(A) Builds new homes.
(B) Paints houses.
(C) Designs interiors.
(D) Provides servants.

87. Who will provide references?

(A) The painters.
(B) The neighbors.
(C) The decorators.
(D) The real estate agents.

88. How long has Carlos been in business?

(A) Four years.
(B) Eight years.
(C) Thirteen years.
(D) Thirty years.

---

89. Who is listening to this announcement?

(A) A football team.
(B) Hospital patients.
(C) Airplane passengers.
(D) A theater audience.

90. How many minutes is the delay?

(A) Five.
(B) Fifteen.
(C) Twenty-five.
(D) Fifty.

91. What does the speaker ask the listeners to do?

(A) Eat.
(B) Smoke.
(C) Sign a document.
(D) Turn off their phones.

---

92. What kind of organization is this?

(A) Sports.
(B) Music.
(C) Youth.
(D) Scholastic.

93. How can a caller get directions to the Center?

(A) Press 2.
(B) Press 4.
(C) Press 9.
(D) Wait until the end of the message.

94. What happens if a caller presses 1?

(A) He can leave a message.
(B) He can get a monthly schedule.
(C) He can find out about tickets.
(D) He can get on the mailing list.

---

95. When will the snowstorm begin?

(A) Wednesday evening.
(B) Friday evening.
(C) Saturday morning.
(D) Saturday afternoon.

96. How much snow will fall?

(A) 2 to 4 inches.
(B) 8 inches.
(C) Less than 10 inches.
(D) 10 to 12 inches.

97. What are listeners advised to do?

(A) Travel.
(B) Stay home.
(C) Turn out the lights.
(D) Drink plenty of water.

---

98. At what time will the first group speaker speak?

(A) 8:45.
(B) 9:15.
(C) 9:30.
(D) 12:00.

99. Where will dinner be served?

(A) In the main meeting room.
(B) In the Red River Room.
(C) In the Blue Mountain Room.
(D) In the club room.

100. What is the new evening activity?

(A) A mountain walk.
(B) A presentation.
(C) A play.
(D) A dance.

This is the end of the Listening test. Turn to Part 5 in your test book.

READING TEST

In the Reading test, you will read a variety of texts and answer several different types of reading comprehension questions. The entire Reading test will last 75 minutes. There are three parts, and directions are given for each part. You are encouraged to answer as many questions as possible within the time allowed.

You must mark your answers on the separate answer sheet. Do not write your answers in the test book.

PART 5

Directions: A word or phrase is missing in each of the sentences below. Four answer choices are given below each sentence. Select the best answer to complete the sentence. Then mark the letter (A), (B), (C), or (D) on your answer sheet.

101. Salary increases will not be higher than the cost of __________.

(A) life
(B) live
(C) living
(D) lived

102. Feel free to __________ the engineer for more assistance.

(A) call on
(B) call to
(C) call forward
(D) call at

103. Mr. Goa __________ the proposal before he looked at the guidelines.

(A) writes
(B) had written
(C) has written
(D) will write

104. If the project is a success, the office __________ more help.

(A) would hire
(B) hired
(C) can hire
(D) could have hired

105. The office manager wants the computers __________ by tomorrow.

(A) will be installed
(B) installing
(C) install
(D) installed

106. Suggestions were requested; __________, none were offered.

(A) in spite of
(B) therefore
(C) however
(D) for this purpose

107. __________ the workers put in a lot of effort, profits were not high.

(A) Whatever
(B) Why
(C) Even though
(D) However

108. The previous __________ of this building was asked to leave because of nonpayment of rent.

(A) defendant
(B) applicant
(C) occupant
(D) assistant

109. Transactions __________.

(A) have weekly been documented
(B) have been documented weekly
(C) weekly have been documented
(D) have been weekly documented

110. Clients are invited to write __________ call for additional information.

(A) but
(B) or
(C) not
(D) either

111. Sylvia was not hired for the position since she didn't have the __________ experience and training.

(A) available
(B) requited
(C) avoidable
(D) requisite

112. The solution cannot be determined __________ the problem is identified.

(A) if
(B) when
(C) until
(D) which

113. The director had her assistant __________ the memo.

(A) signing
(B) signed
(C) will sign
(D) sign

114. If you __________ a touch-tone phone, you won't need an operator.

(A) had
(B) are having
(C) have
(D) will have

115. Our company __________ Metro Messenger Service since 1998.

(A) use
(B) used
(C) had used
(D) has been using

116. The new employees will __________ during training sessions.

(A) catch out
(B) catch on
(C) catch in
(D) catch down

117. The __________ result will be announced next week.

(A) finalized
(B) finally
(C) finalist
(D) final

118. The financing deal is expected to __________ in a matter of weeks.

(A) go up
(B) go out
(C) go through
(D) go beyond

119. The supervisor wants the inventory __________ by next Thursday.

(A) will be finished
(B) finish
(C) finished
(D) finishing

120. I would ask for a special meeting if I __________ her.

(A) was
(B) were
(C) am
(D) would be

121. The company appreciates not only the president's ambition __________ his ideas.

(A) or
(B) but also
(C) with
(D) and if

122. George kindly __________ to pay for my ticket when he saw that I was short of money.

(A) borrowed
(B) purchased
(C) lent
(D) offered

123. The supplier said the department __________ more stock in the future.

(A) has been ordered
(B) order
(C) should order
(D) ordered

124. After reviewing the budget, we realized that we could not __________ to buy a new photocopier this year.

(A) afford
(B) desire
(C) reject
(D) discover

GO ON TO THE NEXT PAGE

125. Sales performance has been poor; __________, the store will close soon.

(A) nevertheless
(B) therefore
(C) on the whole
(D) but

126. Ms. Jacobs is one __________ our best agents.

(A) from
(B) by
(C) of
(D) than

127. Please refer to your personal __________ number.

(A) identify
(B) identities
(C) identification
(D) identified

128. __________ you transfer your account, sign on the dotted line.

(A) While
(B) Because
(C) During
(D) Before

129. No one has turned on the air conditioner __________.

(A) yet
(B) never
(C) already
(D) soon

130. Akinori remained calm __________ his anticipation.

(A) while
(B) in spite of
(C) with
(D) as

131. All bank branches are open __________ 8:30 A.M. to 4:00 P.M.

(A) in
(B) at
(C) from
(D) by

132. We need more details, __________, who, when, what, and where.

(A) for example
(B) moreover
(C) however
(D) accordingly

133. Ms. Simms is very __________ and can always be depended on to fulfill her responsibilities.

(A) reluctant
(B) relievable
(C) reliable
(D) relevant

134. If the company __________ in debt, the accountant would be the first to know.

(A) were
(B) are
(C) would be
(D) will be

135. Who __________ how many offices we have contacted for the survey?

(A) knows
(B) know
(C) is knowing
(D) are knowing

136. There is a rumor that the London office is trying to __________ the Edinburgh office.

(A) take out
(B) take away
(C) take over
(D) take off

137. Before the meeting, a __________ was held to verify information.

(A) brief
(B) briefing
(C) briefly
(D) briefed

138. All staff members will receive an __________ to attend the annual employee appreciation banquet.

(A) invoice
(B) invention
(C) invitation
(D) investment

139. __________ these data before publishing them.

(A) Verification
(B) Verify
(C) Verified
(D) Verifying

140. Either the product __________ the advertisement should be changed.

(A) or
(B) and
(C) but
(D) nor

GO ON TO THE NEXT PAGE

PART 6

Directions: Read the texts that follow. A word or phrase is missing in some of the sentences. Four answer choices are given below each of the sentences. Select the best answer to complete the text. Then mark the letter (A), (B), (C), or (D) on your answer sheet.

Questions 141–143 refer to the following letter.

The Accounting Firm
P.O. Box 90900
Pretoria
0083 South Africa

Alice Michaels
Michaels Enterprises
190 Church Street
Pretoria
0083 South Africa

Dear Mrs. Michaels,

November 7, 20__

I received your e-mail last week, stating that you will not require my services for the upcoming tax year. ________ came as a surprise to me, as I have always provided you

141. (A) Theirs
(B) These
(C) Those
(D) This

with timely service. My records show that your company received a large refund from the government last year.

I understand that you, like many small business owners, ________ to use a

142. (A) have decide
(B) have decision
(C) have decided
(D) have been decided

do-it-yourself tax kit this year. While this method may seem less expensive because it saves money on an accountant's fees, there are hidden costs. It takes a lot of time to gather all the data needed to prepare your own taxes. My firm, on the other hand, already has this information on file, and we know the best ways to save you money on your taxes.

I hope you will think ________ your decision to forego professional accounting

143. (A) up
(B) of
(C) over
(D) after

services this year. If you do change your mind about this, I would be more than happy to provide you with the same efficient and accurate service that I have in years past.

Sincerely,

Peter Jones

GO ON TO THE NEXT PAGE

Questions 144–146 refer to the following e-mail.

To: Reiko Ono
From: Junko Lee
Re: Transfer

Hi Reiko,

I heard the news this morning about your transfer. I was sad to learn that you will be moving to the Yokohama warehouse. It seems like half of the staff is leaving for one reason or another. I considered ________, too, but my

144. (A) transfer
(B) to transfer
(C) transferring
(D) will transfer

husband would never agree to it.

If you need any help packing or making arrangements in Yokohama, let me know. I have many relatives in Yokohama if you and your husband need anywhere to stay for a short time ________ you are looking for a new home. Of course, those

145. (A) while
(B) after
(C) during
(D) before

arrangements may already have been made by the company.

I will miss our conversations in the staff room. You always tell the best stories about your family members, and I feel like I know them personally. I'm sure you will be busy this month, but I'd love to get together for lunch or dinner before you go if you can spare the ________. Tuesdays or Thursdays are the best days for

146. (A) food
(B) place
(C) guests
(D) time

me. If you can't make lunch or dinner, I hope we can at least make one last date for coffee.

Talk to you soon,
Junko

Questions 147–149 refer to the following article.

Korea Daily

International Edition

Maple Home and Life Insurance to Cut 1,500 jobs

The oldest insurance agency in Busan is planning to eliminate at least 1,500 jobs by the end of the year. The mass layoff has already ________, with the first

147. (A) begin
(B) began
(C) begun
(D) beginning

400 people receiving their termination slips last Friday. Maple Home and Life is one of five financial services companies in Korea that has decided to downsize this year. "________ labor costs is the only way we can avoid bankruptcy," said

148. (A) Creating
(B) Building
(C) Operating
(D) Cutting

the company's vice-president.

Financial analyst Yoon Kwang-ung says that an unexpected amount of insurance claims due ________ a season of forest fires, occurring in a weakening

149. (A) to
(B) from
(C) at
(D) in

economy, has caused the mass layoff. But employees are not satisfied with these and other excuses they are hearing in the media. "We want answers. And we won't leave until we get them," said Hwang Woo-suk, who plans to march in a protest outside the insurance office tomorrow.

Questions 150–152 refer to the following letter.

Challenge Media
40, Rue de Suez
13004 Marseille France

Patrice Lerch
Healthy Cereals, Inc.
9, rue Ronchaux
25000 Besançon France

Dear Ms. Lerch: April 5, 20__

We received your request to ________ with our Marseille newspaper

150. (A) write
(B) advertise
(C) photograph
(D) invest

group and are pleased to offer you a full-page spread in three of our papers for the week of April 19. *The Marseille Sun* is a daily paper with distribution in Marseille and surrounding areas. *The Circle* and *The Marseille Bite* are our two local weekly papers. All three of ________ papers cater to middle-class families and business workers.

151. (A) these
(B) theirs
(C) its
(D) ours

Challenge Media charges one flat fee for advertising in all three papers. As well as full-page spreads, you can purchase additional 2-inch squares of advertising in our classified section of *The Marseille Sun.* These options ________ in the price we have quoted you. Please see our website

152. (A) don't include
(B) can't include
(C) aren't included
(D) haven't included

for further information on our classified section (challengemedia.com).

To confirm your order, please call our advertising department at 04.91.88.66. before next Friday.

Thank you for choosing Challenge Media for all of your advertising needs.

Sincerely,

Annie Chateau

Annie Chateau, Managing Director

PART 7

Directions: In this part you will read a selection of texts, such as magazine and newspaper articles, letters, and advertisements. Each text is follwed by several questions. Select the best answer for each question and mark the letter (A), (B), (C), or (D) on your answer sheet.

Questions 153–156 refer to the following memo.

Memorandum

To: Juan Gomez
From: Maria Johnson, Building Engineer
Date: 17 Jan. 20__
Re: Thermostat located in your office

It has come to our attention that the thermostat located in your office is frequently being turned off. Please be aware that although this thermostat is located in your office, it actually controls the temperature on the entire second floor. When it is turned off, it affects not only your office, but all the surrounding offices as well. We ask that you not touch the thermostat. The other second-floor tenants are complaining about the lack of heat in their offices.

If you wish to adjust the temperature in your office at any time, please speak with me or with one of my assistants. We would be happy to help you create an environment that is comfortable for you and your office staff, but please remember that we need to consider the comfort of everyone in the building. Thank you for your cooperation.

153. What is the problem?

(A) Someone keeps turning off the thermostat.
(B) There is no thermostat on the second floor.
(C) The other tenants want a thermostat.
(D) The second floor has enough heat.

154. When should the thermostat be turned off?

(A) In the evenings
(B) When it gets cold out
(C) Never
(D) When it gets hot

155. The word "adjust" in paragraph 2, line 1, is closest in meaning to

(A) pay for
(B) change
(C) look at
(D) open

156. What should Mr. Gomez do?

(A) Change offices
(B) Turn off the heat
(C) Leave the thermostat alone
(D) Complain to the other tenants

Questions 157–159 refer to the following advertisement.

White Shoe Kleen-Kit

White shoes are a handsome addition to any summer wardrobe, but they have always been difficult to keep clean . . . until now. Wright and Perry, the same company that has been providing you with top quality shoe finishes and other fine shoe care products for years, has developed a solution to the problem of cleaning white shoes. Thorough research and careful testing of trial products have resulted in Kleen-Kit, the fantastic new two-step, two-minute product that will keep YOUR white shoes sparkling white. Our special formula not only cleans your shoes to their whitest, it also protects them from dirt and water and preserves the leather, giving your shoes longer life.

If you own a pair of white shoes, or plan to enjoy that extra sparkle that they can add to your wardrobe, this kit is a must. It solves the problem you have always had . . . of keeping white shoes white. And, at a price you can afford.

Kleen-Kit sells for only $7 each, or $5 with each shoe order. Kleen-Kit is available at most shoe retail outlets and anywhere shoe-care products are sold.

Not convinced? Ask your local shoe dealer for a free trial sample or request one from our website. Your shoes will be sparkling white in no time!

157. What is this advertisement promoting?

(A) White shoes
(B) Shoe cleaner
(C) Shoe repair
(D) Company supplies

158. How long does it take to use the kit?

(A) Two minutes
(B) Five minutes
(C) Seven minutes
(D) Ten minutes

159. What problem does the product solve?

(A) Improving Wright shoe sales
(B) Finishing first
(C) Staying handsome
(D) Keeping white shoes white

GO ON TO THE NEXT PAGE

Questions 160–162 refer to the following e-mail.

From: Ms. J. Gibbons
To: All employees
Date: July 17, 20__
Subject: Required hours

All employees are reminded that the Smithson Company observes a 35-hour workweek, normally from 9:00 A.M. to 5:00 P.M., Monday through Friday, with a one-hour lunch period. In addition, after careful consideration and planning, the Smithson Company has recently implemented a flex-time policy. This means that individual employees, with good reason, may establish different work schedules with their supervisor's approval. The employee must explain the reasons for requesting flex-time as well as demonstrate that a variation of work hours will not be detrimental in any way to the work of the other people on that employee's team. Whatever changes may be made to an individual's schedule, 35 hours per week is still expected of all full-time employees.

Flex-time does not mean that an employee can work any hours he or she chooses at any time. In order to make schedule changes under the flex-time policy, an approval form must be submitted to your supervisor two weeks in advance of the proposed schedule change date. The form must be signed and filed by your supervisor before you can start following a new schedule. Forms are available from the Human Resources Office. Employees who adjust their schedule without completing a form and getting formal supervisor approval are subject to loss of pay, even if they work a full 35 hours in a week.

160. What is the topic of the e-mail?

(A) Schedules
(B) Hiring
(C) Observations
(D) Lunches

161. How many hours a week do the employees work?

(A) 17 hours
(B) 25 hours
(C) 35 hours
(D) 40 hours

162. Who must approve any change?

(A) The employee
(B) The employee's supervisor
(C) The human resources director
(D) The vice-president

Questions 163–167 refer to the following memo.

MEMORANDUM

To: All employees
From: George Hendriks, Chief of Security
Date: May 30, 20__
Re: Office Visitors

Employees are reminded that a number of our contracts with clients are of a confidential nature. In order to ensure the maintenance of this confidentiality, visitors will not be allowed within the office area unless they are accompanied by a member of the staff.

Please let your visitors know that they will be asked to sign in at the reception desk when they enter the building. The receptionist will call your office to admit them and give them a visitor's pass. You must come to the reception area and escort your visitors to your office. Unescorted visitors will be asked by security to leave the building.

Thank you for your cooperation with this matter.

163. Who will read this memo?

(A) Clients
(B) Company employees
(C) Visitors
(D) Security staff

164. Why must visitors not be alone?

(A) They may get lost.
(B) They have appointments with staff members.
(C) Company projects are confidential.
(D) They are special guests.

165. What must visitors do when they arrive?

(A) Call the office they are visiting
(B) Admit themselves
(C) Leave before closing
(D) Sign in

166. How will employees know when their visitors have arrived?

(A) The visitors will call ahead.
(B) The receptionist will call the employee's office.
(C) The employee must wait in the reception area.
(D) The visitor will be sent to the employee's office.

167. The word "escort" in paragraph 2, line 4, is closest in meaning to

(A) accompany
(B) remove
(C) invite
(D) hide

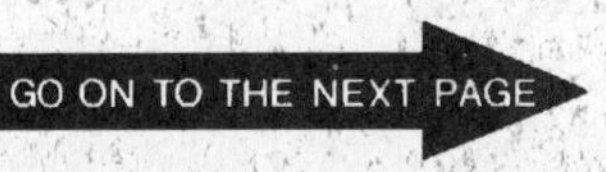

Questions 168–171 refer to the following article.

> Business travelers find that some jobs take them away from home for longer than a few days at a time. Those who find themselves at a new job site for weeks or even months often find it more comfortable and economical to stay at an apartment-hotel rather than a traditional style hotel. The comfort and convenience of these short-term residences are making them more and more popular among frequent business travelers. They provide advantages that more luxurious traditional hotels do not. Apartment-hotels offer both small and full-size apartments that are available to rent on a weekly or monthly basis. Apartments are fully furnished with everything from sofas and writing desks to dishes and silverware. They also usually include cable TV service and Internet access. Best of all, they are run like hotels, with cleaning and linen services, exercise rooms and restaurants, and a desk clerk to take messages and help tenants with questions about the city. In addition, the prices are much more reasonable than the rates normally charged at a traditional hotel. One of the reasons that many apartment-hotels are economically priced is that they are often not found in a city's downtown area. This is not necessarily a disadvantage, however. They are usually conveniently located near public transportation, so the expense of a rental car is not always necessary. In short, apartment-hotels offer a convenient alternative to the business traveler, as they are more cost-effective than traditional hotels and more comfortable than hastily furnished apartments. Many business travelers find that apartment-hotels are as comfortable as it is possible to be away from home.

168. Why are these residences called "apartment-hotels"?

(A) They have characteristics of apartments and hotels.
(B) They contain full-sized apartments.
(C) They look like hotels.
(D) They have only short-term tenants.

169. Who would be likely to use an apartment-hotel?

(A) A businessperson on an overnight trip
(B) A family of tourists
(C) An engineer on a ten-week project away from home
(D) A consultant in town for a convention

170. What is NOT mentioned as an advantage of apartment-hotels?

(A) They are furnished.
(B) They have cleaning service.
(C) They are centrally located.
(D) They have a desk clerk on duty.

171. How do apartment-hotels compare with standard hotels?

(A) The rooms are larger.
(B) They are not as comfortable.
(C) There are fewer services offered.
(D) They are less expensive for a long stay.

Questions 172–174 refer to the following article.

Surveys have found that wages and benefits are not always the major determining factor for employees who are looking to move between jobs. David Bikowski is a case in point. Last year he was laid off from his production job at a factory where he had worked for close to eight years. After several months of searching for a new job, he found employment at another factory in a nearby town. Although he would earn $100 a week less in the new position than he did at his old one, he took the job. He has a family to support and couldn't afford to stay out of work much longer. Just a few months after starting at his new position, he received an offer to return to his old job at his old salary. Bikowski decided to turn the offer down. Why? Because, he says, he finds that his new workplace is much less stressful than the old one. "We've been able to get by on what I've been earning at Strathmore (his new employer), and I know I'll be getting the usual raises as time goes on," he explains. "And it's better for my family in ways that money can't pay for. I'm more relaxed when I get home, I have better quality time with my kids. That's worth more than money to me." Bikowski represents a growing sentiment among the country's workforce. More and more workers are looking for less stressful lives, sociologists say. Work conditions are often given equal weight with wages and benefits when job decisions are made.

172. Why did David Bikowski leave his job?

(A) He wanted a promotion.
(B) He was fired.
(C) He wanted more money.
(D) He was laid off.

173. How does Mr. Bikowski's present salary compare to his salary at his previous job?

(A) It is $100 less a week.
(B) It is $100 less a month.
(C) It is $100 more a week.
(D) It is $100 more a month.

174. According to the article, why did Mr. Bikowski stay at his new job?

(A) The salary is better.
(B) The new job is less stressful.
(C) He has become a supervisor.
(D) He prefers working close to home.

Questions 175–178 refer to the following letter.

GUESS CONSULTING

121 Market St., New York, NY 10012

J. P. Thompson, Esq.
14, Rue du Mont Blanc
1201 Geneva, Switzerland

Dear Mr. Thompson:

I have enclosed a copy of the evaluation that I was hired to prepare for the project "Improving Employee Performance." You will see that the evaluation is divided into three sections, as we agreed upon in our discussion: Employee Relations, Physical Environment, and Training Opportunities. The appendices include all forms and outlines of other methods used to gather information for the evaluation. I have attempted to present everything in as clear a manner as possible. If, however, you have any questions or desire any additional information, please don't hesitate to contact me.

I have enjoyed working with your law firm on this project and look forward to working with you again in the future.

Sincerely,

Amanda Guess

Amanda Guess
Consultant

175. What is the main purpose of the letter?

(A) To submit a report
(B) To inquire about future job possibilities
(C) To request future projects
(D) To ensure prompt payment

176. Which of the following would Mr. Thompson like to improve?

(A) Ms. Guess's writing
(B) Employee performance
(C) The salary
(D) The evaluation

177. According to the letter, which of the following is NOT true?

(A) Ms. Guess would like more projects.
(B) Ms. Guess will discuss her evaluation.
(C) Ms. Guess is a consultant.
(D) Ms. Guess didn't complete the project.

178. What is Mr. Thompson's profession?

(A) Lawyer
(B) Personnel director
(C) Consultant
(D) Landlord

Questions 179–180 refer to the following advertisement.

179. How many time zones can be displayed?

(A) Five
(B) Twelve
(C) Eighteen
(D) Twenty-four

180. How long is the warranty?

(A) Eighteen months
(B) Five years
(C) Eighteen years
(D) Lifetime

GO ON TO THE NEXT PAGE

Questions 181–185 refer to the following letter and e-mail.

Health Center
29 Adelaide St. E.
Toronto, Ontario
Canada
M5A 1N0

Vanessa Wendel
1907 Street Notre-Dame
Montreal, Quebec
Canada
H3A 5T8

Dear Ms. Wendel: January 2, 20__

I understand that you are in charge of the fundraising events for the Heart and Stroke Research Fund of Central Canada. My colleague, Jessica, suggested that I contact you about getting some brochures for our office. We need information on the half marathon that is taking place in Toronto on the weekend of July 1–3.

When I looked at the Heart and Stroke website, I noticed that your name was among the female runners who finished in the top ten last year. Jessica was surprised to hear that in addition to managing the fundraiser, you also participated in the race. You must be in excellent shape! Are you running this year?

I would appreciate your sending some brochures for the center. I'd like to know more about the race myself. I've been thinking about entering, but I'm not sure if I am ready to run a half marathon. I think I should start with a ten-kilometer run. Currently I run about 20 kilometers each week.

Hope to hear from you soon.

Best Wishes,

Kandy Miller

Kandy Miller, Front Office Manager

To: Kandy Miller
From: Vanessa Wendel
Subject: Marathon Brochures

Hi Kandy,

Thank you for your letter. It was fun participating in the race last year. At first when my co-workers decided to do the run I wasn't interested. However, within a few weeks of their training I noticed how much more energy they had. That's when I decided to join them. It was a good experience, but unfortunately I will not be running in this year's event. I pulled a muscle in my leg when I was golfing this summer. You should give this run a try, though. It took me about 6 months to train for the half marathon. It will probably take you half of that since you have some running experience already.

I sent some brochures to the Health Center today. Thank you for your support of our cause. Last year we raised $400,000 in Toronto, and this year our goal is to double that amount.

Thanks again,
Vanessa

Vanessa Wendel
Fundraising Supervisor

181. Why did Miller write this letter?

(A) To request sponsorship money
(B) To explain about a fundraiser
(C) To order some brochures
(D) To ask for advice about exercise

182. How far will participants in the July race have to run?

(A) A full marathon
(B) A half marathon
(C) 10 kilometers
(D) 20 kilometers

183. Why isn't Wendel running at this year's event?

(A) She has a golf engagement.
(B) She has a sore leg.
(C) She has low energy.
(D) She has a running injury.

184. If Miller started training immediately, when would she be ready for the run according to Wendel?

(A) By January
(B) By April
(C) In 6 months
(D) Around July 3

185. How much money do they want to raise at the Toronto running event this year?

(A) $200,000
(B) $400,000
(C) $800,000
(D) $1,200,000

GO ON TO THE NEXT PAGE

Questions 186–190 refer to the following e-mail and advertisement.

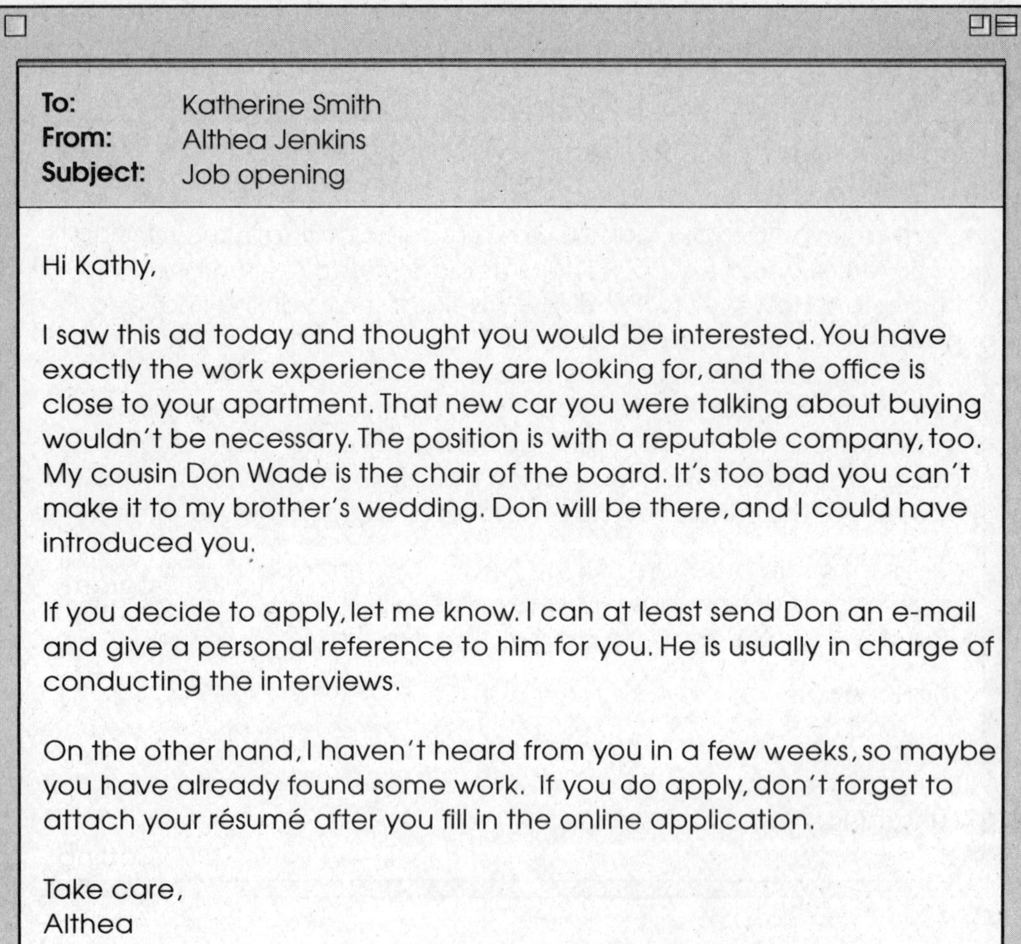

To: Katherine Smith
From: Althea Jenkins
Subject: Job opening

Hi Kathy,

I saw this ad today and thought you would be interested. You have exactly the work experience they are looking for, and the office is close to your apartment. That new car you were talking about buying wouldn't be necessary. The position is with a reputable company, too. My cousin Don Wade is the chair of the board. It's too bad you can't make it to my brother's wedding. Don will be there, and I could have introduced you.

If you decide to apply, let me know. I can at least send Don an e-mail and give a personal reference to him for you. He is usually in charge of conducting the interviews.

On the other hand, I haven't heard from you in a few weeks, so maybe you have already found some work. If you do apply, don't forget to attach your résumé after you fill in the online application.

Take care,
Althea

You are reviewing JOB BANK item #334885. To apply to this ad and attach an electronic résumé, click here.

Job Opening
Pharmacy Assistant
Part-time

Harrison's Pharmaceutical Company and Store—Auckland

Job Description:

- Provide clerical support to four pharmacists who have rotating shifts
- Measure, mix, and package prescription drugs*
- Take care of computer inventory and restocking
- Update customer files

Note: This position does not involve patient counseling or taking telephone prescriptions.

Qualifications and requirements:

- ✔ 2 years' experience under a licensed pharmacist
- ✔ Pharmacy Assistance License A
- ✔ Certificate from an accredited Pharmacy Assistant Program

Hours: Monday–Friday 9 A.M.–1 P.M.
Salary: Negotiable
Health Benefits: Not applicable

*Some deliveries may be required. No car is necessary.

How to apply for this job:
Please send a cover letter and résumé to the above JOB BANK number. We will respond within 10 days if we are interested in setting up an interview. Please copy and paste your résumé into the blank file provided. Do not send e-mail attachments.

186. Which is true about Althea's brother?

(A) He is the chair of a board.
(B) He is getting married.
(C) He noticed this ad.
(D) He needs to find a job.

187. What is Althea unsure of?

(A) Whether or not Kathy still needs a job
(B) When Kathy wants to go back to work
(C) Where Kathy and her kids live
(D) Whether or not Wade will be at the wedding

188. What does Kathy NOT need in order to apply for this job?

(A) A Pharmacy Assistant's license
(B) A vehicle for making deliveries
(C) Experience in a pharmacy
(D) A license to work in a pharmacy

189. Why does Althea think Kathy is suitable for this job?

(A) Kathy is buying a new car anyway.
(B) Kathy knows some of the staff members already.
(C) Kathy has two years' experience working in a pharmacy.
(D Kathy only wants to work part time.

190. What advice does Althea give that Kathy must ignore if she wants the job?

(A) Look at the JOB BANK ad
(B) Fill out the online application
(C) Attend Althea's brother's wedding
(D) Attach her résumé to her e-mail

GO ON TO THE NEXT PAGE

Questions 191–195 refer to the following notice and e-mail message.

NOTICE

The four parking garages for Mansfield Towers will be closed at various times during the last three weeks of June for cleaning and repainting. Please make alternative arrangements for parking during this period. Make sure to inform the receptionist in the lobby if you are expecting clients from out of town in June. We will issue temporary parking passes for the garage at 5th and Main for our clients. These passes can be purchased for a fee of $2.00 a day during the month of June, but are reserved for regular clients, not employees. There are five spots available for these clients, and these will be assigned on a reservation basis only.

Note: Parking on Green St. or Howe Ave. is strictly prohibited. Cars that are illegally parked will be ticketed and towed. For information about other local parking garages call the city help line at 800-555-9000.

To: Niels Henrikson
From: Eva Pederson
Subject: Conference parking
Date: June 2

Hi Niels,

Have you seen the notice in the parking garage? I'm really concerned because I'm organizing the conference we have coming up in the middle of this month and I don't know what to do about parking for everyone. So far, at least 50 potential clients have committed to attending the conference and 30 more haven't responded to the invitation yet. I expect at least 60, possibly more, will attend, but I don't know where they're all going to park since the garage will be closed. There's that garage on Calvin Street that I think is open on weekends, but it's at least a ten-minute walk from here. I don't think that would make a very good first impression, considering that any of the conference attendees may one day become important clients. Do you have any ideas about this?

Thanks,

Eva

191. Where in Mansfield Towers was this notice posted?

(A) In the parking garage
(B) In the lobby
(C) In the conference room
(D) In the elevator

192. What ideas might Henrikson offer to Pederson if he checks the notice?

(A) They could call the city for parking advice.
(B) They could make a reservation with the receptionist.
(C) They could ask clients not to forget their passes.
(D) They could each give up an employee pass.

193. Why are none of the people attending the conference allowed to park at the 5th and Main garage?

(A) They didn't make reservations on time.
(B) They aren't current clients.
(C) They only have temporary passes.
(D) They are from out of town.

194. When is the conference taking place?

(A) Over a weekend
(B) The first week of June
(C) In the middle of June
(D) In ten minutes

195. How many attendees does Pederson expect at the conference?

(A) less than 30
(B) less than 50
(C) about 60
(D) over 80

GO ON TO THE NEXT PAGE

Questions 196–200 refer to the following advertisement and e-mail.

Taipei Discount Package Deals

You are viewing our online Hotel and Air Packages

Travel valid from September 10 to December 1*

Tokyo Comfort Zone Inn

Room includes:

- Four-star rating
- 1 single bed
- Internet access and satellite television

Location:

Ten-minute walk from Tokyo International Airport
Free shuttle bus available.

**Conditions:*

From October 2 to 4 there is a black-out period for this deal. No reservations will be taken during this time.

Click here to bookmark this site.
TAIPEI DISCOUNT PACKAGE DEALS
Managed by TP Discount Travel Agency, Ltd.
Travel Agent License No: 22009

To: Geo Friends
From: Kit-ken Lim
Re: Itinerary

To Whom It May Concern,

Below you will find my travel itinerary. Again, I'm sorry that I wasn't able to book my trip for the weekend of the 3rd as you requested. That weekend would have been perfect for me as well. I leave Tokyo at 4 P.M. on the 10th. Unless I hear from you before I leave, I will assume that one of you will meet me at the airport with a sign. I have never been to Tokyo before, so I would prefer not to have to hire a taxi or find my own way to the hotel. I look forward to discussing franchise opportunities and to meeting all of you. I will have my checkbook with me in case we work out a deal right away.

Thank you,

Kit-ken Lim

P.S. I'll be wearing a green hat and a long black coat.

To: Kit-ken Lim
From: Geo Friends
Re: Itinerary

Name: Kit-ken Lim
Departure: Chiang Kai-shek. 9:30 A.M. October 7
Arrival: Tokyo. 1 P.M. October 7
Hotel Accommodations: Tokyo Comfort Zone Inn; 3 nights
Style of occupancy: Double
Total cost including taxes: Not applicable.
*Paid in full using air travel points

196. Why does Lim apologize in his e-mail?

(A) A black-out period changed his travel plans.
(B) He was busy on the weekend of the 3rd.
(C) He forgot to book his return flight.
(D) It is his first time traveling to Tokyo.

197. How does Lim plan to get to the hotel from the airport?

(A) He will take a shuttle bus.
(B) He will hire a taxi.
(C) He will walk the short distance.
(D) He will be picked up.

198. What type of travel was booked?

(A) A business trip
(B) A vacation
(C) A group tour
(D) A study trip

199. How does Lim's reservation differ from the original ad?

(A) He decided to stay in a 4-star hotel.
(B) He requested a room with a television.
(C) He switched to a double room.
(D) He chose a different travel agency.

200. How was this trip paid for?

(A) With travel points
(B) With a credit card
(C) With cash
(D) With a check

This is the end of the test. If you finish before time is called, you may go back to Parts 5, 6, and 7 and check your work.

ANSWER SHEETS

ANSWER SHEET: Practice Test One

Name ____________________

Listening Comprehension

Part 1 | Part 2 | Part 3 | Part 4

	Answer A B C D		Answer A B C		Answer A B C		Answer A B C		Answer A B C D		Answer A B C D		Answer A B C D		Answer A B C D		Answer A B C D		Answer A B C D
1	Ⓐ Ⓑ Ⓒ Ⓓ	11	Ⓐ Ⓑ Ⓒ	21	Ⓐ Ⓑ Ⓒ	31	Ⓐ Ⓑ Ⓒ	41	Ⓐ Ⓑ Ⓒ Ⓓ	51	Ⓐ Ⓑ Ⓒ Ⓓ	61	Ⓐ Ⓑ Ⓒ Ⓓ	71	Ⓐ Ⓑ Ⓒ Ⓓ	81	Ⓐ Ⓑ Ⓒ Ⓓ	91	Ⓐ Ⓑ Ⓒ Ⓓ
2	Ⓐ Ⓑ Ⓒ Ⓓ	12	Ⓐ Ⓑ Ⓒ	22	Ⓐ Ⓑ Ⓒ	32	Ⓐ Ⓑ Ⓒ	42	Ⓐ Ⓑ Ⓒ Ⓓ	52	Ⓐ Ⓑ Ⓒ Ⓓ	62	Ⓐ Ⓑ Ⓒ Ⓓ	72	Ⓐ Ⓑ Ⓒ Ⓓ	82	Ⓐ Ⓑ Ⓒ Ⓓ	92	Ⓐ Ⓑ Ⓒ Ⓓ
3	Ⓐ Ⓑ Ⓒ Ⓓ	13	Ⓐ Ⓑ Ⓒ	23	Ⓐ Ⓑ Ⓒ	33	Ⓐ Ⓑ Ⓒ	43	Ⓐ Ⓑ Ⓒ Ⓓ	53	Ⓐ Ⓑ Ⓒ Ⓓ	63	Ⓐ Ⓑ Ⓒ Ⓓ	73	Ⓐ Ⓑ Ⓒ Ⓓ	83	Ⓐ Ⓑ Ⓒ Ⓓ	93	Ⓐ Ⓑ Ⓒ Ⓓ
4	Ⓐ Ⓑ Ⓒ Ⓓ	14	Ⓐ Ⓑ Ⓒ	24	Ⓐ Ⓑ Ⓒ	34	Ⓐ Ⓑ Ⓒ	44	Ⓐ Ⓑ Ⓒ Ⓓ	54	Ⓐ Ⓑ Ⓒ Ⓓ	64	Ⓐ Ⓑ Ⓒ Ⓓ	74	Ⓐ Ⓑ Ⓒ Ⓓ	84	Ⓐ Ⓑ Ⓒ Ⓓ	94	Ⓐ Ⓑ Ⓒ Ⓓ
5	Ⓐ Ⓑ Ⓒ Ⓓ	15	Ⓐ Ⓑ Ⓒ	25	Ⓐ Ⓑ Ⓒ	35	Ⓐ Ⓑ Ⓒ	45	Ⓐ Ⓑ Ⓒ Ⓓ	55	Ⓐ Ⓑ Ⓒ Ⓓ	65	Ⓐ Ⓑ Ⓒ Ⓓ	75	Ⓐ Ⓑ Ⓒ Ⓓ	85	Ⓐ Ⓑ Ⓒ Ⓓ	95	Ⓐ Ⓑ Ⓒ Ⓓ
6	Ⓐ Ⓑ Ⓒ Ⓓ	16	Ⓐ Ⓑ Ⓒ	26	Ⓐ Ⓑ Ⓒ	36	Ⓐ Ⓑ Ⓒ	46	Ⓐ Ⓑ Ⓒ Ⓓ	56	Ⓐ Ⓑ Ⓒ Ⓓ	66	Ⓐ Ⓑ Ⓒ Ⓓ	76	Ⓐ Ⓑ Ⓒ Ⓓ	86	Ⓐ Ⓑ Ⓒ Ⓓ	96	Ⓐ Ⓑ Ⓒ Ⓓ
7	Ⓐ Ⓑ Ⓒ Ⓓ	17	Ⓐ Ⓑ Ⓒ	27	Ⓐ Ⓑ Ⓒ	37	Ⓐ Ⓑ Ⓒ	47	Ⓐ Ⓑ Ⓒ Ⓓ	57	Ⓐ Ⓑ Ⓒ Ⓓ	67	Ⓐ Ⓑ Ⓒ Ⓓ	77	Ⓐ Ⓑ Ⓒ Ⓓ	87	Ⓐ Ⓑ Ⓒ Ⓓ	97	Ⓐ Ⓑ Ⓒ Ⓓ
8	Ⓐ Ⓑ Ⓒ Ⓓ	18	Ⓐ Ⓑ Ⓒ	28	Ⓐ Ⓑ Ⓒ	38	Ⓐ Ⓑ Ⓒ	48	Ⓐ Ⓑ Ⓒ Ⓓ	58	Ⓐ Ⓑ Ⓒ Ⓓ	68	Ⓐ Ⓑ Ⓒ Ⓓ	78	Ⓐ Ⓑ Ⓒ Ⓓ	88	Ⓐ Ⓑ Ⓒ Ⓓ	98	Ⓐ Ⓑ Ⓒ Ⓓ
9	Ⓐ Ⓑ Ⓒ Ⓓ	19	Ⓐ Ⓑ Ⓒ	29	Ⓐ Ⓑ Ⓒ	39	Ⓐ Ⓑ Ⓒ	49	Ⓐ Ⓑ Ⓒ Ⓓ	59	Ⓐ Ⓑ Ⓒ Ⓓ	69	Ⓐ Ⓑ Ⓒ Ⓓ	79	Ⓐ Ⓑ Ⓒ Ⓓ	89	Ⓐ Ⓑ Ⓒ Ⓓ	99	Ⓐ Ⓑ Ⓒ Ⓓ
10	Ⓐ Ⓑ Ⓒ Ⓓ	20	Ⓐ Ⓑ Ⓒ	30	Ⓐ Ⓑ Ⓒ	40	Ⓐ Ⓑ Ⓒ	50	Ⓐ Ⓑ Ⓒ Ⓓ	60	Ⓐ Ⓑ Ⓒ Ⓓ	70	Ⓐ Ⓑ Ⓒ Ⓓ	80	Ⓐ Ⓑ Ⓒ Ⓓ	90	Ⓐ Ⓑ Ⓒ Ⓓ	100	Ⓐ Ⓑ Ⓒ Ⓓ

Reading

Part 5 | Part 6 | Part 7

	Answer A B C D		Answer A B C D		Answer A B C D		Answer A B C D		Answer A B C D		Answer A B C D		Answer A B C D		Answer A B C D		Answer A B C D		Answer A B C D
101	Ⓐ Ⓑ Ⓒ Ⓓ	111	Ⓐ Ⓑ Ⓒ Ⓓ	121	Ⓐ Ⓑ Ⓒ Ⓓ	131	Ⓐ Ⓑ Ⓒ Ⓓ	141	Ⓐ Ⓑ Ⓒ Ⓓ	151	Ⓐ Ⓑ Ⓒ Ⓓ	161	Ⓐ Ⓑ Ⓒ Ⓓ	171	Ⓐ Ⓑ Ⓒ Ⓓ	181	Ⓐ Ⓑ Ⓒ Ⓓ	191	Ⓐ Ⓑ Ⓒ Ⓓ
102	Ⓐ Ⓑ Ⓒ Ⓓ	112	Ⓐ Ⓑ Ⓒ Ⓓ	122	Ⓐ Ⓑ Ⓒ Ⓓ	132	Ⓐ Ⓑ Ⓒ Ⓓ	142	Ⓐ Ⓑ Ⓒ Ⓓ	152	Ⓐ Ⓑ Ⓒ Ⓓ	162	Ⓐ Ⓑ Ⓒ Ⓓ	172	Ⓐ Ⓑ Ⓒ Ⓓ	182	Ⓐ Ⓑ Ⓒ Ⓓ	192	Ⓐ Ⓑ Ⓒ Ⓓ
103	Ⓐ Ⓑ Ⓒ Ⓓ	113	Ⓐ Ⓑ Ⓒ Ⓓ	123	Ⓐ Ⓑ Ⓒ Ⓓ	133	Ⓐ Ⓑ Ⓒ Ⓓ	143	Ⓐ Ⓑ Ⓒ Ⓓ	153	Ⓐ Ⓑ Ⓒ Ⓓ	163	Ⓐ Ⓑ Ⓒ Ⓓ	173	Ⓐ Ⓑ Ⓒ Ⓓ	183	Ⓐ Ⓑ Ⓒ Ⓓ	193	Ⓐ Ⓑ Ⓒ Ⓓ
104	Ⓐ Ⓑ Ⓒ Ⓓ	114	Ⓐ Ⓑ Ⓒ Ⓓ	124	Ⓐ Ⓑ Ⓒ Ⓓ	134	Ⓐ Ⓑ Ⓒ Ⓓ	144	Ⓐ Ⓑ Ⓒ Ⓓ	154	Ⓐ Ⓑ Ⓒ Ⓓ	164	Ⓐ Ⓑ Ⓒ Ⓓ	174	Ⓐ Ⓑ Ⓒ Ⓓ	184	Ⓐ Ⓑ Ⓒ Ⓓ	194	Ⓐ Ⓑ Ⓒ Ⓓ
105	Ⓐ Ⓑ Ⓒ Ⓓ	115	Ⓐ Ⓑ Ⓒ Ⓓ	125	Ⓐ Ⓑ Ⓒ Ⓓ	135	Ⓐ Ⓑ Ⓒ Ⓓ	145	Ⓐ Ⓑ Ⓒ Ⓓ	155	Ⓐ Ⓑ Ⓒ Ⓓ	165	Ⓐ Ⓑ Ⓒ Ⓓ	175	Ⓐ Ⓑ Ⓒ Ⓓ	185	Ⓐ Ⓑ Ⓒ Ⓓ	195	Ⓐ Ⓑ Ⓒ Ⓓ
106	Ⓐ Ⓑ Ⓒ Ⓓ	116	Ⓐ Ⓑ Ⓒ Ⓓ	126	Ⓐ Ⓑ Ⓒ Ⓓ	136	Ⓐ Ⓑ Ⓒ Ⓓ	146	Ⓐ Ⓑ Ⓒ Ⓓ	156	Ⓐ Ⓑ Ⓒ Ⓓ	166	Ⓐ Ⓑ Ⓒ Ⓓ	176	Ⓐ Ⓑ Ⓒ Ⓓ	186	Ⓐ Ⓑ Ⓒ Ⓓ	196	Ⓐ Ⓑ Ⓒ Ⓓ
107	Ⓐ Ⓑ Ⓒ Ⓓ	117	Ⓐ Ⓑ Ⓒ Ⓓ	127	Ⓐ Ⓑ Ⓒ Ⓓ	137	Ⓐ Ⓑ Ⓒ Ⓓ	147	Ⓐ Ⓑ Ⓒ Ⓓ	157	Ⓐ Ⓑ Ⓒ Ⓓ	167	Ⓐ Ⓑ Ⓒ Ⓓ	177	Ⓐ Ⓑ Ⓒ Ⓓ	187	Ⓐ Ⓑ Ⓒ Ⓓ	197	Ⓐ Ⓑ Ⓒ Ⓓ
108	Ⓐ Ⓑ Ⓒ Ⓓ	118	Ⓐ Ⓑ Ⓒ Ⓓ	128	Ⓐ Ⓑ Ⓒ Ⓓ	138	Ⓐ Ⓑ Ⓒ Ⓓ	148	Ⓐ Ⓑ Ⓒ Ⓓ	158	Ⓐ Ⓑ Ⓒ Ⓓ	168	Ⓐ Ⓑ Ⓒ Ⓓ	178	Ⓐ Ⓑ Ⓒ Ⓓ	188	Ⓐ Ⓑ Ⓒ Ⓓ	198	Ⓐ Ⓑ Ⓒ Ⓓ
109	Ⓐ Ⓑ Ⓒ Ⓓ	119	Ⓐ Ⓑ Ⓒ Ⓓ	129	Ⓐ Ⓑ Ⓒ Ⓓ	139	Ⓐ Ⓑ Ⓒ Ⓓ	149	Ⓐ Ⓑ Ⓒ Ⓓ	159	Ⓐ Ⓑ Ⓒ Ⓓ	169	Ⓐ Ⓑ Ⓒ Ⓓ	179	Ⓐ Ⓑ Ⓒ Ⓓ	189	Ⓐ Ⓑ Ⓒ Ⓓ	199	Ⓐ Ⓑ Ⓒ Ⓓ
110	Ⓐ Ⓑ Ⓒ Ⓓ	120	Ⓐ Ⓑ Ⓒ Ⓓ	130	Ⓐ Ⓑ Ⓒ Ⓓ	140	Ⓐ Ⓑ Ⓒ Ⓓ	150	Ⓐ Ⓑ Ⓒ Ⓓ	160	Ⓐ Ⓑ Ⓒ Ⓓ	170	Ⓐ Ⓑ Ⓒ Ⓓ	180	Ⓐ Ⓑ Ⓒ Ⓓ	190	Ⓐ Ⓑ Ⓒ Ⓓ	200	Ⓐ Ⓑ Ⓒ Ⓓ

ANSWER SHEET: Practice Test Two

Name ____________________

Listening Comprehension

Part 1 · Part 2 · Part 3 · Part 4

	Answer A B C D		Answer A B C		Answer A B C		Answer A B C		Answer A B C D		Answer A B C D		Answer A B C D		Answer A B C D		Answer A B C D		Answer A B C D
1	Ⓐ Ⓑ Ⓒ Ⓓ	11	Ⓐ Ⓑ Ⓒ	21	Ⓐ Ⓑ Ⓒ	31	Ⓐ Ⓑ Ⓒ	41	Ⓐ Ⓑ Ⓒ Ⓓ	51	Ⓐ Ⓑ Ⓒ Ⓓ	61	Ⓐ Ⓑ Ⓒ Ⓓ	71	Ⓐ Ⓑ Ⓒ Ⓓ	81	Ⓐ Ⓑ Ⓒ Ⓓ	91	Ⓐ Ⓑ Ⓒ Ⓓ
2	Ⓐ Ⓑ Ⓒ Ⓓ	12	Ⓐ Ⓑ Ⓒ	22	Ⓐ Ⓑ Ⓒ	32	Ⓐ Ⓑ Ⓒ	42	Ⓐ Ⓑ Ⓒ Ⓓ	52	Ⓐ Ⓑ Ⓒ Ⓓ	62	Ⓐ Ⓑ Ⓒ Ⓓ	72	Ⓐ Ⓑ Ⓒ Ⓓ	82	Ⓐ Ⓑ Ⓒ Ⓓ	92	Ⓐ Ⓑ Ⓒ Ⓓ
3	Ⓐ Ⓑ Ⓒ Ⓓ	13	Ⓐ Ⓑ Ⓒ	23	Ⓐ Ⓑ Ⓒ	33	Ⓐ Ⓑ Ⓒ	43	Ⓐ Ⓑ Ⓒ Ⓓ	53	Ⓐ Ⓑ Ⓒ Ⓓ	63	Ⓐ Ⓑ Ⓒ Ⓓ	73	Ⓐ Ⓑ Ⓒ Ⓓ	83	Ⓐ Ⓑ Ⓒ Ⓓ	93	Ⓐ Ⓑ Ⓒ Ⓓ
4	Ⓐ Ⓑ Ⓒ Ⓓ	14	Ⓐ Ⓑ Ⓒ	24	Ⓐ Ⓑ Ⓒ	34	Ⓐ Ⓑ Ⓒ	44	Ⓐ Ⓑ Ⓒ Ⓓ	54	Ⓐ Ⓑ Ⓒ Ⓓ	64	Ⓐ Ⓑ Ⓒ Ⓓ	74	Ⓐ Ⓑ Ⓒ Ⓓ	84	Ⓐ Ⓑ Ⓒ Ⓓ	94	Ⓐ Ⓑ Ⓒ Ⓓ
5	Ⓐ Ⓑ Ⓒ Ⓓ	15	Ⓐ Ⓑ Ⓒ	25	Ⓐ Ⓑ Ⓒ	35	Ⓐ Ⓑ Ⓒ	45	Ⓐ Ⓑ Ⓒ Ⓓ	55	Ⓐ Ⓑ Ⓒ Ⓓ	65	Ⓐ Ⓑ Ⓒ Ⓓ	75	Ⓐ Ⓑ Ⓒ Ⓓ	85	Ⓐ Ⓑ Ⓒ Ⓓ	95	Ⓐ Ⓑ Ⓒ Ⓓ
6	Ⓐ Ⓑ Ⓒ Ⓓ	16	Ⓐ Ⓑ Ⓒ	26	Ⓐ Ⓑ Ⓒ	36	Ⓐ Ⓑ Ⓒ	46	Ⓐ Ⓑ Ⓒ Ⓓ	56	Ⓐ Ⓑ Ⓒ Ⓓ	66	Ⓐ Ⓑ Ⓒ Ⓓ	76	Ⓐ Ⓑ Ⓒ Ⓓ	86	Ⓐ Ⓑ Ⓒ Ⓓ	96	Ⓐ Ⓑ Ⓒ Ⓓ
7	Ⓐ Ⓑ Ⓒ Ⓓ	17	Ⓐ Ⓑ Ⓒ	27	Ⓐ Ⓑ Ⓒ	37	Ⓐ Ⓑ Ⓒ	47	Ⓐ Ⓑ Ⓒ Ⓓ	57	Ⓐ Ⓑ Ⓒ Ⓓ	67	Ⓐ Ⓑ Ⓒ Ⓓ	77	Ⓐ Ⓑ Ⓒ Ⓓ	87	Ⓐ Ⓑ Ⓒ Ⓓ	97	Ⓐ Ⓑ Ⓒ Ⓓ
8	Ⓐ Ⓑ Ⓒ Ⓓ	18	Ⓐ Ⓑ Ⓒ	28	Ⓐ Ⓑ Ⓒ	38	Ⓐ Ⓑ Ⓒ	48	Ⓐ Ⓑ Ⓒ Ⓓ	58	Ⓐ Ⓑ Ⓒ Ⓓ	68	Ⓐ Ⓑ Ⓒ Ⓓ	78	Ⓐ Ⓑ Ⓒ Ⓓ	88	Ⓐ Ⓑ Ⓒ Ⓓ	98	Ⓐ Ⓑ Ⓒ Ⓓ
9	Ⓐ Ⓑ Ⓒ Ⓓ	19	Ⓐ Ⓑ Ⓒ	29	Ⓐ Ⓑ Ⓒ	39	Ⓐ Ⓑ Ⓒ	49	Ⓐ Ⓑ Ⓒ Ⓓ	59	Ⓐ Ⓑ Ⓒ Ⓓ	69	Ⓐ Ⓑ Ⓒ Ⓓ	79	Ⓐ Ⓑ Ⓒ Ⓓ	89	Ⓐ Ⓑ Ⓒ Ⓓ	99	Ⓐ Ⓑ Ⓒ Ⓓ
10	Ⓐ Ⓑ Ⓒ Ⓓ	20	Ⓐ Ⓑ Ⓒ	30	Ⓐ Ⓑ Ⓒ	40	Ⓐ Ⓑ Ⓒ	50	Ⓐ Ⓑ Ⓒ Ⓓ	60	Ⓐ Ⓑ Ⓒ Ⓓ	70	Ⓐ Ⓑ Ⓒ Ⓓ	80	Ⓐ Ⓑ Ⓒ Ⓓ	90	Ⓐ Ⓑ Ⓒ Ⓓ	100	Ⓐ Ⓑ Ⓒ Ⓓ

Reading

Part 5 · Part 6 · Part 7

	Answer A B C D		Answer A B C D		Answer A B C D		Answer A B C D		Answer A B C D		Answer A B C D		Answer A B C D		Answer A B C D		Answer A B C D		Answer A B C D
101	Ⓐ Ⓑ Ⓒ Ⓓ	111	Ⓐ Ⓑ Ⓒ Ⓓ	121	Ⓐ Ⓑ Ⓒ Ⓓ	131	Ⓐ Ⓑ Ⓒ Ⓓ	141	Ⓐ Ⓑ Ⓒ Ⓓ	151	Ⓐ Ⓑ Ⓒ Ⓓ	161	Ⓐ Ⓑ Ⓒ Ⓓ	171	Ⓐ Ⓑ Ⓒ Ⓓ	181	Ⓐ Ⓑ Ⓒ Ⓓ	191	Ⓐ Ⓑ Ⓒ Ⓓ
102	Ⓐ Ⓑ Ⓒ Ⓓ	112	Ⓐ Ⓑ Ⓒ Ⓓ	122	Ⓐ Ⓑ Ⓒ Ⓓ	132	Ⓐ Ⓑ Ⓒ Ⓓ	142	Ⓐ Ⓑ Ⓒ Ⓓ	152	Ⓐ Ⓑ Ⓒ Ⓓ	162	Ⓐ Ⓑ Ⓒ Ⓓ	172	Ⓐ Ⓑ Ⓒ Ⓓ	182	Ⓐ Ⓑ Ⓒ Ⓓ	192	Ⓐ Ⓑ Ⓒ Ⓓ
103	Ⓐ Ⓑ Ⓒ Ⓓ	113	Ⓐ Ⓑ Ⓒ Ⓓ	123	Ⓐ Ⓑ Ⓒ Ⓓ	133	Ⓐ Ⓑ Ⓒ Ⓓ	143	Ⓐ Ⓑ Ⓒ Ⓓ	153	Ⓐ Ⓑ Ⓒ Ⓓ	163	Ⓐ Ⓑ Ⓒ Ⓓ	173	Ⓐ Ⓑ Ⓒ Ⓓ	183	Ⓐ Ⓑ Ⓒ Ⓓ	193	Ⓐ Ⓑ Ⓒ Ⓓ
104	Ⓐ Ⓑ Ⓒ Ⓓ	114	Ⓐ Ⓑ Ⓒ Ⓓ	124	Ⓐ Ⓑ Ⓒ Ⓓ	134	Ⓐ Ⓑ Ⓒ Ⓓ	144	Ⓐ Ⓑ Ⓒ Ⓓ	154	Ⓐ Ⓑ Ⓒ Ⓓ	164	Ⓐ Ⓑ Ⓒ Ⓓ	174	Ⓐ Ⓑ Ⓒ Ⓓ	184	Ⓐ Ⓑ Ⓒ Ⓓ	194	Ⓐ Ⓑ Ⓒ Ⓓ
105	Ⓐ Ⓑ Ⓒ Ⓓ	115	Ⓐ Ⓑ Ⓒ Ⓓ	125	Ⓐ Ⓑ Ⓒ Ⓓ	135	Ⓐ Ⓑ Ⓒ Ⓓ	145	Ⓐ Ⓑ Ⓒ Ⓓ	155	Ⓐ Ⓑ Ⓒ Ⓓ	165	Ⓐ Ⓑ Ⓒ Ⓓ	175	Ⓐ Ⓑ Ⓒ Ⓓ	185	Ⓐ Ⓑ Ⓒ Ⓓ	195	Ⓐ Ⓑ Ⓒ Ⓓ
106	Ⓐ Ⓑ Ⓒ Ⓓ	116	Ⓐ Ⓑ Ⓒ Ⓓ	126	Ⓐ Ⓑ Ⓒ Ⓓ	136	Ⓐ Ⓑ Ⓒ Ⓓ	146	Ⓐ Ⓑ Ⓒ Ⓓ	156	Ⓐ Ⓑ Ⓒ Ⓓ	166	Ⓐ Ⓑ Ⓒ Ⓓ	176	Ⓐ Ⓑ Ⓒ Ⓓ	186	Ⓐ Ⓑ Ⓒ Ⓓ	196	Ⓐ Ⓑ Ⓒ Ⓓ
107	Ⓐ Ⓑ Ⓒ Ⓓ	117	Ⓐ Ⓑ Ⓒ Ⓓ	127	Ⓐ Ⓑ Ⓒ Ⓓ	137	Ⓐ Ⓑ Ⓒ Ⓓ	147	Ⓐ Ⓑ Ⓒ Ⓓ	157	Ⓐ Ⓑ Ⓒ Ⓓ	167	Ⓐ Ⓑ Ⓒ Ⓓ	177	Ⓐ Ⓑ Ⓒ Ⓓ	187	Ⓐ Ⓑ Ⓒ Ⓓ	197	Ⓐ Ⓑ Ⓒ Ⓓ
108	Ⓐ Ⓑ Ⓒ Ⓓ	118	Ⓐ Ⓑ Ⓒ Ⓓ	128	Ⓐ Ⓑ Ⓒ Ⓓ	138	Ⓐ Ⓑ Ⓒ Ⓓ	148	Ⓐ Ⓑ Ⓒ Ⓓ	158	Ⓐ Ⓑ Ⓒ Ⓓ	168	Ⓐ Ⓑ Ⓒ Ⓓ	178	Ⓐ Ⓑ Ⓒ Ⓓ	188	Ⓐ Ⓑ Ⓒ Ⓓ	198	Ⓐ Ⓑ Ⓒ Ⓓ
109	Ⓐ Ⓑ Ⓒ Ⓓ	119	Ⓐ Ⓑ Ⓒ Ⓓ	129	Ⓐ Ⓑ Ⓒ Ⓓ	139	Ⓐ Ⓑ Ⓒ Ⓓ	149	Ⓐ Ⓑ Ⓒ Ⓓ	159	Ⓐ Ⓑ Ⓒ Ⓓ	169	Ⓐ Ⓑ Ⓒ Ⓓ	179	Ⓐ Ⓑ Ⓒ Ⓓ	189	Ⓐ Ⓑ Ⓒ Ⓓ	199	Ⓐ Ⓑ Ⓒ Ⓓ
110	Ⓐ Ⓑ Ⓒ Ⓓ	120	Ⓐ Ⓑ Ⓒ Ⓓ	130	Ⓐ Ⓑ Ⓒ Ⓓ	140	Ⓐ Ⓑ Ⓒ Ⓓ	150	Ⓐ Ⓑ Ⓒ Ⓓ	160	Ⓐ Ⓑ Ⓒ Ⓓ	170	Ⓐ Ⓑ Ⓒ Ⓓ	180	Ⓐ Ⓑ Ⓒ Ⓓ	190	Ⓐ Ⓑ Ⓒ Ⓓ	200	Ⓐ Ⓑ Ⓒ Ⓓ

ANSWER SHEET: Practice Test Three

Name ______________________

Listening Comprehension

Part 1 · Part 2 · Part 3 · Part 4

	Answer		Answer		Answer		Answer		Answer		Answer		Answer		Answer		Answer		Answer
	A B C D		A B C		A B C		A B C		A B C D		A B C D		A B C D		A B C D		A B C D		A B C D
1	Ⓐ Ⓑ Ⓒ Ⓓ	11	Ⓐ Ⓑ Ⓒ	21	Ⓐ Ⓑ Ⓒ	31	Ⓐ Ⓑ Ⓒ	41	Ⓐ Ⓑ Ⓒ Ⓓ	51	Ⓐ Ⓑ Ⓒ Ⓓ	61	Ⓐ Ⓑ Ⓒ Ⓓ	71	Ⓐ Ⓑ Ⓒ Ⓓ	81	Ⓐ Ⓑ Ⓒ Ⓓ	91	Ⓐ Ⓑ Ⓒ Ⓓ
2	Ⓐ Ⓑ Ⓒ Ⓓ	12	Ⓐ Ⓑ Ⓒ	22	Ⓐ Ⓑ Ⓒ	32	Ⓐ Ⓑ Ⓒ	42	Ⓐ Ⓑ Ⓒ Ⓓ	52	Ⓐ Ⓑ Ⓒ Ⓓ	62	Ⓐ Ⓑ Ⓒ Ⓓ	72	Ⓐ Ⓑ Ⓒ Ⓓ	82	Ⓐ Ⓑ Ⓒ Ⓓ	92	Ⓐ Ⓑ Ⓒ Ⓓ
3	Ⓐ Ⓑ Ⓒ Ⓓ	13	Ⓐ Ⓑ Ⓒ	23	Ⓐ Ⓑ Ⓒ	33	Ⓐ Ⓑ Ⓒ	43	Ⓐ Ⓑ Ⓒ Ⓓ	53	Ⓐ Ⓑ Ⓒ Ⓓ	63	Ⓐ Ⓑ Ⓒ Ⓓ	73	Ⓐ Ⓑ Ⓒ Ⓓ	83	Ⓐ Ⓑ Ⓒ Ⓓ	93	Ⓐ Ⓑ Ⓒ Ⓓ
4	Ⓐ Ⓑ Ⓒ Ⓓ	14	Ⓐ Ⓑ Ⓒ	24	Ⓐ Ⓑ Ⓒ	34	Ⓐ Ⓑ Ⓒ	44	Ⓐ Ⓑ Ⓒ Ⓓ	54	Ⓐ Ⓑ Ⓒ Ⓓ	64	Ⓐ Ⓑ Ⓒ Ⓓ	74	Ⓐ Ⓑ Ⓒ Ⓓ	84	Ⓐ Ⓑ Ⓒ Ⓓ	94	Ⓐ Ⓑ Ⓒ Ⓓ
5	Ⓐ Ⓑ Ⓒ Ⓓ	15	Ⓐ Ⓑ Ⓒ	25	Ⓐ Ⓑ Ⓒ	35	Ⓐ Ⓑ Ⓒ	45	Ⓐ Ⓑ Ⓒ Ⓓ	55	Ⓐ Ⓑ Ⓒ Ⓓ	65	Ⓐ Ⓑ Ⓒ Ⓓ	75	Ⓐ Ⓑ Ⓒ Ⓓ	85	Ⓐ Ⓑ Ⓒ Ⓓ	95	Ⓐ Ⓑ Ⓒ Ⓓ
6	Ⓐ Ⓑ Ⓒ Ⓓ	16	Ⓐ Ⓑ Ⓒ	26	Ⓐ Ⓑ Ⓒ	36	Ⓐ Ⓑ Ⓒ	46	Ⓐ Ⓑ Ⓒ Ⓓ	56	Ⓐ Ⓑ Ⓒ Ⓓ	66	Ⓐ Ⓑ Ⓒ Ⓓ	76	Ⓐ Ⓑ Ⓒ Ⓓ	86	Ⓐ Ⓑ Ⓒ Ⓓ	96	Ⓐ Ⓑ Ⓒ Ⓓ
7	Ⓐ Ⓑ Ⓒ Ⓓ	17	Ⓐ Ⓑ Ⓒ	27	Ⓐ Ⓑ Ⓒ	37	Ⓐ Ⓑ Ⓒ	47	Ⓐ Ⓑ Ⓒ Ⓓ	57	Ⓐ Ⓑ Ⓒ Ⓓ	67	Ⓐ Ⓑ Ⓒ Ⓓ	77	Ⓐ Ⓑ Ⓒ Ⓓ	87	Ⓐ Ⓑ Ⓒ Ⓓ	97	Ⓐ Ⓑ Ⓒ Ⓓ
8	Ⓐ Ⓑ Ⓒ Ⓓ	18	Ⓐ Ⓑ Ⓒ	28	Ⓐ Ⓑ Ⓒ	38	Ⓐ Ⓑ Ⓒ	48	Ⓐ Ⓑ Ⓒ Ⓓ	58	Ⓐ Ⓑ Ⓒ Ⓓ	68	Ⓐ Ⓑ Ⓒ Ⓓ	78	Ⓐ Ⓑ Ⓒ Ⓓ	88	Ⓐ Ⓑ Ⓒ Ⓓ	98	Ⓐ Ⓑ Ⓒ Ⓓ
9	Ⓐ Ⓑ Ⓒ Ⓓ	19	Ⓐ Ⓑ Ⓒ	29	Ⓐ Ⓑ Ⓒ	39	Ⓐ Ⓑ Ⓒ	49	Ⓐ Ⓑ Ⓒ Ⓓ	59	Ⓐ Ⓑ Ⓒ Ⓓ	69	Ⓐ Ⓑ Ⓒ Ⓓ	79	Ⓐ Ⓑ Ⓒ Ⓓ	89	Ⓐ Ⓑ Ⓒ Ⓓ	99	Ⓐ Ⓑ Ⓒ Ⓓ
10	Ⓐ Ⓑ Ⓒ Ⓓ	20	Ⓐ Ⓑ Ⓒ	30	Ⓐ Ⓑ Ⓒ	40	Ⓐ Ⓑ Ⓒ	50	Ⓐ Ⓑ Ⓒ Ⓓ	60	Ⓐ Ⓑ Ⓒ Ⓓ	70	Ⓐ Ⓑ Ⓒ Ⓓ	80	Ⓐ Ⓑ Ⓒ Ⓓ	90	Ⓐ Ⓑ Ⓒ Ⓓ	100	Ⓐ Ⓑ Ⓒ Ⓓ

Reading

Part 5 · Part 6 · Part 7

	Answer		Answer		Answer		Answer		Answer		Answer		Answer		Answer		Answer		Answer
	A B C D		A B C D		A B C D		A B C D		A B C D		A B C D		A B C D		A B C D		A B C D		A B C D
101	Ⓐ Ⓑ Ⓒ Ⓓ	111	Ⓐ Ⓑ Ⓒ Ⓓ	121	Ⓐ Ⓑ Ⓒ Ⓓ	131	Ⓐ Ⓑ Ⓒ Ⓓ	141	Ⓐ Ⓑ Ⓒ Ⓓ	151	Ⓐ Ⓑ Ⓒ Ⓓ	161	Ⓐ Ⓑ Ⓒ Ⓓ	171	Ⓐ Ⓑ Ⓒ Ⓓ	181	Ⓐ Ⓑ Ⓒ Ⓓ	191	Ⓐ Ⓑ Ⓒ Ⓓ
102	Ⓐ Ⓑ Ⓒ Ⓓ	112	Ⓐ Ⓑ Ⓒ Ⓓ	122	Ⓐ Ⓑ Ⓒ Ⓓ	132	Ⓐ Ⓑ Ⓒ Ⓓ	142	Ⓐ Ⓑ Ⓒ Ⓓ	152	Ⓐ Ⓑ Ⓒ Ⓓ	162	Ⓐ Ⓑ Ⓒ Ⓓ	172	Ⓐ Ⓑ Ⓒ Ⓓ	182	Ⓐ Ⓑ Ⓒ Ⓓ	192	Ⓐ Ⓑ Ⓒ Ⓓ
103	Ⓐ Ⓑ Ⓒ Ⓓ	113	Ⓐ Ⓑ Ⓒ Ⓓ	123	Ⓐ Ⓑ Ⓒ Ⓓ	133	Ⓐ Ⓑ Ⓒ Ⓓ	143	Ⓐ Ⓑ Ⓒ Ⓓ	153	Ⓐ Ⓑ Ⓒ Ⓓ	163	Ⓐ Ⓑ Ⓒ Ⓓ	173	Ⓐ Ⓑ Ⓒ Ⓓ	183	Ⓐ Ⓑ Ⓒ Ⓓ	193	Ⓐ Ⓑ Ⓒ Ⓓ
104	Ⓐ Ⓑ Ⓒ Ⓓ	114	Ⓐ Ⓑ Ⓒ Ⓓ	124	Ⓐ Ⓑ Ⓒ Ⓓ	134	Ⓐ Ⓑ Ⓒ Ⓓ	144	Ⓐ Ⓑ Ⓒ Ⓓ	154	Ⓐ Ⓑ Ⓒ Ⓓ	164	Ⓐ Ⓑ Ⓒ Ⓓ	174	Ⓐ Ⓑ Ⓒ Ⓓ	184	Ⓐ Ⓑ Ⓒ Ⓓ	194	Ⓐ Ⓑ Ⓒ Ⓓ
105	Ⓐ Ⓑ Ⓒ Ⓓ	115	Ⓐ Ⓑ Ⓒ Ⓓ	125	Ⓐ Ⓑ Ⓒ Ⓓ	135	Ⓐ Ⓑ Ⓒ Ⓓ	145	Ⓐ Ⓑ Ⓒ Ⓓ	155	Ⓐ Ⓑ Ⓒ Ⓓ	165	Ⓐ Ⓑ Ⓒ Ⓓ	175	Ⓐ Ⓑ Ⓒ Ⓓ	185	Ⓐ Ⓑ Ⓒ Ⓓ	195	Ⓐ Ⓑ Ⓒ Ⓓ
106	Ⓐ Ⓑ Ⓒ Ⓓ	116	Ⓐ Ⓑ Ⓒ Ⓓ	126	Ⓐ Ⓑ Ⓒ Ⓓ	136	Ⓐ Ⓑ Ⓒ Ⓓ	146	Ⓐ Ⓑ Ⓒ Ⓓ	156	Ⓐ Ⓑ Ⓒ Ⓓ	166	Ⓐ Ⓑ Ⓒ Ⓓ	176	Ⓐ Ⓑ Ⓒ Ⓓ	186	Ⓐ Ⓑ Ⓒ Ⓓ	196	Ⓐ Ⓑ Ⓒ Ⓓ
107	Ⓐ Ⓑ Ⓒ Ⓓ	117	Ⓐ Ⓑ Ⓒ Ⓓ	127	Ⓐ Ⓑ Ⓒ Ⓓ	137	Ⓐ Ⓑ Ⓒ Ⓓ	147	Ⓐ Ⓑ Ⓒ Ⓓ	157	Ⓐ Ⓑ Ⓒ Ⓓ	167	Ⓐ Ⓑ Ⓒ Ⓓ	177	Ⓐ Ⓑ Ⓒ Ⓓ	187	Ⓐ Ⓑ Ⓒ Ⓓ	197	Ⓐ Ⓑ Ⓒ Ⓓ
108	Ⓐ Ⓑ Ⓒ Ⓓ	118	Ⓐ Ⓑ Ⓒ Ⓓ	128	Ⓐ Ⓑ Ⓒ Ⓓ	138	Ⓐ Ⓑ Ⓒ Ⓓ	148	Ⓐ Ⓑ Ⓒ Ⓓ	158	Ⓐ Ⓑ Ⓒ Ⓓ	168	Ⓐ Ⓑ Ⓒ Ⓓ	178	Ⓐ Ⓑ Ⓒ Ⓓ	188	Ⓐ Ⓑ Ⓒ Ⓓ	198	Ⓐ Ⓑ Ⓒ Ⓓ
109	Ⓐ Ⓑ Ⓒ Ⓓ	119	Ⓐ Ⓑ Ⓒ Ⓓ	129	Ⓐ Ⓑ Ⓒ Ⓓ	139	Ⓐ Ⓑ Ⓒ Ⓓ	149	Ⓐ Ⓑ Ⓒ Ⓓ	159	Ⓐ Ⓑ Ⓒ Ⓓ	169	Ⓐ Ⓑ Ⓒ Ⓓ	179	Ⓐ Ⓑ Ⓒ Ⓓ	189	Ⓐ Ⓑ Ⓒ Ⓓ	199	Ⓐ Ⓑ Ⓒ Ⓓ
110	Ⓐ Ⓑ Ⓒ Ⓓ	120	Ⓐ Ⓑ Ⓒ Ⓓ	130	Ⓐ Ⓑ Ⓒ Ⓓ	140	Ⓐ Ⓑ Ⓒ Ⓓ	150	Ⓐ Ⓑ Ⓒ Ⓓ	160	Ⓐ Ⓑ Ⓒ Ⓓ	170	Ⓐ Ⓑ Ⓒ Ⓓ	180	Ⓐ Ⓑ Ⓒ Ⓓ	190	Ⓐ Ⓑ Ⓒ Ⓓ	200	Ⓐ Ⓑ Ⓒ Ⓓ

ANSWER SHEET: Practice Test Four

Name ____________________

Listening Comprehension

Part 1 / Part 2 / Part 3 / Part 4

	Answer		Answer		Answer		Answer		Answer		Answer		Answer		Answer		Answer		Answer
	A B C D		A B C		A B C		A B C		A B C D				A B C D		A B C D		A B C D		A B C D
1	Ⓐ Ⓑ Ⓒ Ⓓ	11	Ⓐ Ⓑ Ⓒ	21	Ⓐ Ⓑ Ⓒ	31	Ⓐ Ⓑ Ⓒ	41	Ⓐ Ⓑ Ⓒ Ⓓ	51	Ⓐ Ⓑ Ⓒ Ⓓ	61	Ⓐ Ⓑ Ⓒ Ⓓ	71	Ⓐ Ⓑ Ⓒ Ⓓ	81	Ⓐ Ⓑ Ⓒ Ⓓ	91	Ⓐ Ⓑ Ⓒ Ⓓ
2	Ⓐ Ⓑ Ⓒ Ⓓ	12	Ⓐ Ⓑ Ⓒ	22	Ⓐ Ⓑ Ⓒ	32	Ⓐ Ⓑ Ⓒ	42	Ⓐ Ⓑ Ⓒ Ⓓ	52	Ⓐ Ⓑ Ⓒ Ⓓ	62	Ⓐ Ⓑ Ⓒ Ⓓ	72	Ⓐ Ⓑ Ⓒ Ⓓ	82	Ⓐ Ⓑ Ⓒ Ⓓ	92	Ⓐ Ⓑ Ⓒ Ⓓ
3	Ⓐ Ⓑ Ⓒ Ⓓ	13	Ⓐ Ⓑ Ⓒ	23	Ⓐ Ⓑ Ⓒ	33	Ⓐ Ⓑ Ⓒ	43	Ⓐ Ⓑ Ⓒ Ⓓ	53	Ⓐ Ⓑ Ⓒ Ⓓ	63	Ⓐ Ⓑ Ⓒ Ⓓ	73	Ⓐ Ⓑ Ⓒ Ⓓ	83	Ⓐ Ⓑ Ⓒ Ⓓ	93	Ⓐ Ⓑ Ⓒ Ⓓ
4	Ⓐ Ⓑ Ⓒ Ⓓ	14	Ⓐ Ⓑ Ⓒ	24	Ⓐ Ⓑ Ⓒ	34	Ⓐ Ⓑ Ⓒ	44	Ⓐ Ⓑ Ⓒ Ⓓ	54	Ⓐ Ⓑ Ⓒ Ⓓ	64	Ⓐ Ⓑ Ⓒ Ⓓ	74	Ⓐ Ⓑ Ⓒ Ⓓ	84	Ⓐ Ⓑ Ⓒ Ⓓ	94	Ⓐ Ⓑ Ⓒ Ⓓ
5	Ⓐ Ⓑ Ⓒ Ⓓ	15	Ⓐ Ⓑ Ⓒ	25	Ⓐ Ⓑ Ⓒ	35	Ⓐ Ⓑ Ⓒ	45	Ⓐ Ⓑ Ⓒ Ⓓ	55	Ⓐ Ⓑ Ⓒ Ⓓ	65	Ⓐ Ⓑ Ⓒ Ⓓ	75	Ⓐ Ⓑ Ⓒ Ⓓ	85	Ⓐ Ⓑ Ⓒ Ⓓ	95	Ⓐ Ⓑ Ⓒ Ⓓ
6	Ⓐ Ⓑ Ⓒ Ⓓ	16	Ⓐ Ⓑ Ⓒ	26	Ⓐ Ⓑ Ⓒ	36	Ⓐ Ⓑ Ⓒ	46	Ⓐ Ⓑ Ⓒ Ⓓ	56	Ⓐ Ⓑ Ⓒ Ⓓ	66	Ⓐ Ⓑ Ⓒ Ⓓ	76	Ⓐ Ⓑ Ⓒ Ⓓ	86	Ⓐ Ⓑ Ⓒ Ⓓ	96	Ⓐ Ⓑ Ⓒ Ⓓ
7	Ⓐ Ⓑ Ⓒ Ⓓ	17	Ⓐ Ⓑ Ⓒ	27	Ⓐ Ⓑ Ⓒ	37	Ⓐ Ⓑ Ⓒ	47	Ⓐ Ⓑ Ⓒ Ⓓ	57	Ⓐ Ⓑ Ⓒ Ⓓ	67	Ⓐ Ⓑ Ⓒ Ⓓ	77	Ⓐ Ⓑ Ⓒ Ⓓ	87	Ⓐ Ⓑ Ⓒ Ⓓ	97	Ⓐ Ⓑ Ⓒ Ⓓ
8	Ⓐ Ⓑ Ⓒ Ⓓ	18	Ⓐ Ⓑ Ⓒ	28	Ⓐ Ⓑ Ⓒ	38	Ⓐ Ⓑ Ⓒ	48	Ⓐ Ⓑ Ⓒ Ⓓ	58	Ⓐ Ⓑ Ⓒ Ⓓ	68	Ⓐ Ⓑ Ⓒ Ⓓ	78	Ⓐ Ⓑ Ⓒ Ⓓ	88	Ⓐ Ⓑ Ⓒ Ⓓ	98	Ⓐ Ⓑ Ⓒ Ⓓ
9	Ⓐ Ⓑ Ⓒ Ⓓ	19	Ⓐ Ⓑ Ⓒ	29	Ⓐ Ⓑ Ⓒ	39	Ⓐ Ⓑ Ⓒ	49	Ⓐ Ⓑ Ⓒ Ⓓ	59	Ⓐ Ⓑ Ⓒ Ⓓ	69	Ⓐ Ⓑ Ⓒ Ⓓ	79	Ⓐ Ⓑ Ⓒ Ⓓ	89	Ⓐ Ⓑ Ⓒ Ⓓ	99	Ⓐ Ⓑ Ⓒ Ⓓ
10	Ⓐ Ⓑ Ⓒ Ⓓ	20	Ⓐ Ⓑ Ⓒ	30	Ⓐ Ⓑ Ⓒ	40	Ⓐ Ⓑ Ⓒ	50	Ⓐ Ⓑ Ⓒ Ⓓ	60	Ⓐ Ⓑ Ⓒ Ⓓ	70	Ⓐ Ⓑ Ⓒ Ⓓ	80	Ⓐ Ⓑ Ⓒ Ⓓ	90	Ⓐ Ⓑ Ⓒ Ⓓ	100	Ⓐ Ⓑ Ⓒ Ⓓ

Reading

Part 5 / Part 6 / Part 7

	Answer		Answer		Answer		Answer		Answer		Answer		Answer		Answer		Answer		Answer
	A B C D		A B C D		A B C D		A B C D		A B C D		A B C D		A B C D		A B C D		A B C D		A B C D
101	Ⓐ Ⓑ Ⓒ Ⓓ	111	Ⓐ Ⓑ Ⓒ Ⓓ	121	Ⓐ Ⓑ Ⓒ Ⓓ	131	Ⓐ Ⓑ Ⓒ Ⓓ	141	Ⓐ Ⓑ Ⓒ Ⓓ	151	Ⓐ Ⓑ Ⓒ Ⓓ	161	Ⓐ Ⓑ Ⓒ Ⓓ	171	Ⓐ Ⓑ Ⓒ Ⓓ	181	Ⓐ Ⓑ Ⓒ Ⓓ	191	Ⓐ Ⓑ Ⓒ Ⓓ
102	Ⓐ Ⓑ Ⓒ Ⓓ	112	Ⓐ Ⓑ Ⓒ Ⓓ	122	Ⓐ Ⓑ Ⓒ Ⓓ	132	Ⓐ Ⓑ Ⓒ Ⓓ	142	Ⓐ Ⓑ Ⓒ Ⓓ	152	Ⓐ Ⓑ Ⓒ Ⓓ	162	Ⓐ Ⓑ Ⓒ Ⓓ	172	Ⓐ Ⓑ Ⓒ Ⓓ	182	Ⓐ Ⓑ Ⓒ Ⓓ	192	Ⓐ Ⓑ Ⓒ Ⓓ
103	Ⓐ Ⓑ Ⓒ Ⓓ	113	Ⓐ Ⓑ Ⓒ Ⓓ	123	Ⓐ Ⓑ Ⓒ Ⓓ	133	Ⓐ Ⓑ Ⓒ Ⓓ	143	Ⓐ Ⓑ Ⓒ Ⓓ	153	Ⓐ Ⓑ Ⓒ Ⓓ	163	Ⓐ Ⓑ Ⓒ Ⓓ	173	Ⓐ Ⓑ Ⓒ Ⓓ	183	Ⓐ Ⓑ Ⓒ Ⓓ	193	Ⓐ Ⓑ Ⓒ Ⓓ
104	Ⓐ Ⓑ Ⓒ Ⓓ	114	Ⓐ Ⓑ Ⓒ Ⓓ	124	Ⓐ Ⓑ Ⓒ Ⓓ	134	Ⓐ Ⓑ Ⓒ Ⓓ	144	Ⓐ Ⓑ Ⓒ Ⓓ	154	Ⓐ Ⓑ Ⓒ Ⓓ	164	Ⓐ Ⓑ Ⓒ Ⓓ	174	Ⓐ Ⓑ Ⓒ Ⓓ	184	Ⓐ Ⓑ Ⓒ Ⓓ	194	Ⓐ Ⓑ Ⓒ Ⓓ
105	Ⓐ Ⓑ Ⓒ Ⓓ	115	Ⓐ Ⓑ Ⓒ Ⓓ	125	Ⓐ Ⓑ Ⓒ Ⓓ	135	Ⓐ Ⓑ Ⓒ Ⓓ	145	Ⓐ Ⓑ Ⓒ Ⓓ	155	Ⓐ Ⓑ Ⓒ Ⓓ	165	Ⓐ Ⓑ Ⓒ Ⓓ	175	Ⓐ Ⓑ Ⓒ Ⓓ	185	Ⓐ Ⓑ Ⓒ Ⓓ	195	Ⓐ Ⓑ Ⓒ Ⓓ
106	Ⓐ Ⓑ Ⓒ Ⓓ	116	Ⓐ Ⓑ Ⓒ Ⓓ	126	Ⓐ Ⓑ Ⓒ Ⓓ	136	Ⓐ Ⓑ Ⓒ Ⓓ	146	Ⓐ Ⓑ Ⓒ Ⓓ	156	Ⓐ Ⓑ Ⓒ Ⓓ	166	Ⓐ Ⓑ Ⓒ Ⓓ	176	Ⓐ Ⓑ Ⓒ Ⓓ	186	Ⓐ Ⓑ Ⓒ Ⓓ	196	Ⓐ Ⓑ Ⓒ Ⓓ
107	Ⓐ Ⓑ Ⓒ Ⓓ	117	Ⓐ Ⓑ Ⓒ Ⓓ	127	Ⓐ Ⓑ Ⓒ Ⓓ	137	Ⓐ Ⓑ Ⓒ Ⓓ	147	Ⓐ Ⓑ Ⓒ Ⓓ	157	Ⓐ Ⓑ Ⓒ Ⓓ	167	Ⓐ Ⓑ Ⓒ Ⓓ	177	Ⓐ Ⓑ Ⓒ Ⓓ	187	Ⓐ Ⓑ Ⓒ Ⓓ	197	Ⓐ Ⓑ Ⓒ Ⓓ
108	Ⓐ Ⓑ Ⓒ Ⓓ	118	Ⓐ Ⓑ Ⓒ Ⓓ	128	Ⓐ Ⓑ Ⓒ Ⓓ	138	Ⓐ Ⓑ Ⓒ Ⓓ	148	Ⓐ Ⓑ Ⓒ Ⓓ	158	Ⓐ Ⓑ Ⓒ Ⓓ	168	Ⓐ Ⓑ Ⓒ Ⓓ	178	Ⓐ Ⓑ Ⓒ Ⓓ	188	Ⓐ Ⓑ Ⓒ Ⓓ	198	Ⓐ Ⓑ Ⓒ Ⓓ
109	Ⓐ Ⓑ Ⓒ Ⓓ	119	Ⓐ Ⓑ Ⓒ Ⓓ	129	Ⓐ Ⓑ Ⓒ Ⓓ	139	Ⓐ Ⓑ Ⓒ Ⓓ	149	Ⓐ Ⓑ Ⓒ Ⓓ	159	Ⓐ Ⓑ Ⓒ Ⓓ	169	Ⓐ Ⓑ Ⓒ Ⓓ	179	Ⓐ Ⓑ Ⓒ Ⓓ	189	Ⓐ Ⓑ Ⓒ Ⓓ	199	Ⓐ Ⓑ Ⓒ Ⓓ
110	Ⓐ Ⓑ Ⓒ Ⓓ	120	Ⓐ Ⓑ Ⓒ Ⓓ	130	Ⓐ Ⓑ Ⓒ Ⓓ	140	Ⓐ Ⓑ Ⓒ Ⓓ	150	Ⓐ Ⓑ Ⓒ Ⓓ	160	Ⓐ Ⓑ Ⓒ Ⓓ	170	Ⓐ Ⓑ Ⓒ Ⓓ	180	Ⓐ Ⓑ Ⓒ Ⓓ	190	Ⓐ Ⓑ Ⓒ Ⓓ	200	Ⓐ Ⓑ Ⓒ Ⓓ

Practice Test Score Conversion

HOW TO CONVERT YOUR PRACTICE TEST SCORES

To convert your practice test scores, use the table on page 176. Follow these simple steps.

1. Take a practice test.
2. Total the number of correct answers in the listening section.
3. Match the total number of correct listening answers with the corresponding practice score.
4. Total the number of correct answers in the reading section.
5. Match the total number of correct reading answers with the corresponding practice score.
6. Add the two scores together. This is your estimated total practice score.

Sample
Number of correct listening answers 56 = Practice listening score 290
Number of correct reading answers 82 = Practice reading score + 405
Estimated total practice score 695

Your score on Practice Test 1
Number of correct listening answers ____ = Practice listening score ______
Number of correct reading answers ____ = Practice reading score +______
Estimated total practice score ______

Your score on Practice Test 2
Number of correct listening answers ____ = Practice listening score ______
Number of correct reading answers ____ = Practice reading score +______
Estimated total practice score ______

Your score on Practice Test 3
Number of correct listening answers ____ = Practice listening score ______
Number of correct reading answers ____ = Practice reading score +______
Estimated total practice score ______

Your score on Practice Test 4
Number of correct listening answers ____ = Practice listening score ______
Number of correct reading answers ____ = Practice reading score +______
Estimated total practice score ______

PRACTICE TEST ESTIMATED SCORE CONVERSION TABLE

	PRACTICE SCORE	
# CORRECT	LISTENING	READING
0	5	5
1	5	5
2	5	5
3	5	5
4	5	5
5	5	5
6	5	5
7	10	5
8	15	5
9	20	5
10	25	5
11	30	5
12	35	5
13	40	5
14	45	5
15	50	5
16	55	10
17	60	15
18	65	20
19	70	25
20	75	30
21	80	35
22	85	40
23	90	45
24	95	50
25	100	60
26	110	65
27	115	70
28	120	80
29	125	85
30	130	90
31	135	95
32	140	100
33	145	110
34	150	115
35	160	120
36	165	125
37	170	130
38	175	140
39	180	145
40	185	150
41	190	160
42	195	165
43	200	170
44	210	175
45	215	180
46	220	190
47	230	195
48	240	200
49	245	210
50	250	215

	PRACTICE SCORE	
# CORRECT	LISTENING	READING
51	255	220
52	260	225
53	270	230
54	275	235
55	280	240
56	290	250
57	295	255
58	300	260
59	310	265
60	315	270
61	320	280
62	325	285
63	330	290
64	340	300
65	345	305
66	350	310
67	360	320
68	365	325
69	370	330
70	380	335
71	385	340
72	390	350
73	395	355
74	400	360
75	405	365
76	410	370
77	420	380
78	425	385
79	430	390
80	440	395
81	445	400
82	450	405
83	460	410
84	465	415
85	470	420
86	475	425
87	480	430
88	485	435
89	490	445
90	495	450
91	495	455
92	495	465
93	495	470
94	495	480
95	495	485
96	495	490
97	495	495
98	495	495
99	495	495
100	495	495

CD-ROM CONTENTS

MP3 AUDIO FILES FOR THE COMPLETE AUDIO PROGRAM:

Practice Test 1, Listening Parts 1–4 (CD 1, tracks 2–28)
Practice Test 2, Listening Parts 1–4 (CD 2, tracks 2–28)
Practice Test 3, Listening Parts 1–4 (CD 3, tracks 2–28)
Practice Test 4, Listening Parts 1–4 (CD 4, tracks 2–28)

PDF FILES FOR:

Complete Audioscript
Complete Answer Key